INDIAN CULTURES
OF THE AMERICAN SOUTHWEST

BY STEVEN L. WALKER

Above: Freshly fallen snow covers Pueblo del Arroyo at Chaco Culture National Historic Park in New Mexico.
PHOTO BY GEORGE H. H. HUEY

Above: Anasazi granary and Kachina Bridge in Natural Bridges National Monument, Utah.
PHOTO BY GEORGE H. H. HUEY

 CAMELBACK
GROUP, INCORPORATED

 CANYONLANDS
PUBLICATIONS & INDIAN ART

Designed by Camelback Design Group, Inc., 6625 North Scottsdale Road, Scottsdale, Arizona 85250. Telephone: 602-948-4233. Distributed by Canyonlands Publications, 4999 East Empire, Unit A, Flagstaff, Arizona 86004. For ordering information please call (602) 527-0730.

Library of Congress Catalog Number: 93-072733
International Standard Book Number: 1-879924-10-2

 Proudly printed and bound in the U.S.A.

Front Cover:
Square Tower House, Mesa Verde National Park.
PHOTO BY JEFF GNASS
Top Inset: Projectile points from Homolovi ruins.
PHOTO BY MICHAEL COLLIER
Bottom Inset: Hopi kachina dolls.
PHOTO BY JERRY JACKA

Left: Montezuma Castle, Montezuma Castle National Monument, Arizona.
PHOTO BY GEORGE H. H. HUEY

Back Cover: Antelope House Ruin, Canyon del Muerto, Canyon de Chelly National Monument.
PHOTO BY JEFF GNASS

Inside Back Cover: Betatakin Ruin in winter, Navajo National Monument, Arizona.
PHOTO BY GEORGE H. H. HUEY

INTRODUCTION

Early Paleo-Indian hunters and gatherers left paintings and carvings on rocks and cliff walls that depicted the important events in their lives. These early nomadic groups evolved into more sedentary cultures; the remains of their pithouses, pueblos and cliff dwellings giving an insight into their daily lives. The first Europeans to arrive in the Southwest, Spanish conquistadors searching for material wealth, forever changed the Indian's role in the region, leaving a legacy of abusing the native inhabitants. After the Anglo-American westward migration brought their civilization to the Southwest, the Indians were relegated to life on the reservations.

Migrating from Asia via an ancient land bridge across the Bering Strait during the Pleistocene Epoch, or Ice Age, at least 37,000 years ago, the earliest inhabitants of the Southwest were true men who walked erect, possessed fire, wore clothing of fur and skin, and used tools made of flint and bone. The exposed land bridge between the continents allowed grazing animals, and hunters who preyed on them, access to the New World. Migrations lasted until the end of the Ice Age, around 11,000 years ago.

These early inhabitants pursued elephants, mastodons, mammoths, giant sloths, camels, horses and prehistoric bison (around twice the size and about four times the weight of those found in recorded history). It is believed they led their nomadic existence in the New World for several thousand years before disappearing from the archeological record. They were replaced, or assimilated, by distinctly Asian tribes who bore no resemblance to the earlier inhabitants, but were also big game hunters.

The first of these early Asian tribes to reach the Southwest, more than 12,000 years ago, are known as the Big Game Hunters or the Elephant Hunters. Climactic conditions in the Southwest were far more tropical than today: a juniper savanna covered the arid desert near Las Vegas, Nevada; a savanna of pine and spruce, dotted with lakes, filled the now treeless plains of the Llano Estacado in eastern New Mexico and Texas; and Late Pleistocene streams flowed throughout the Southwest.

Paleo-Indian hunters depended on hunting the larger prehistoric beasts. Using organized teamwork to hunt, they fashioned spearheads of stone with detachable foreshafts. The shafts detached after entering the prey and animals could not easily work the embedded points from wounds, which hastened their deaths.

As the polar ice caps melted, the Southwest's climate became increasingly drier between 8000 and 7000 B.C., causing a decrease in annual rainfall of three to four inches and an increase in mean annual temperature between three and four degrees. Lush vegetation the larger mammals depended on for survival became increasingly scarce, as did the animals themselves. Final extinction of mammoths, mastodons, camels, elephants, horses and other large species may have been hastened by the Big Game Hunters themselves as they struggled to find the last of the diminishing herds to support their bands. Consequently, the Big Game Hunters themselves disappeared.

It is uncertain whether the next inhabitants to appear, Paleo-Indians (evidenced by the discovery of complexes including the Clovis culture, dating earlier than 9000 B.C.; Folsom culture, slightly after 9000 B.C.; Agate Basin culture around 8000 B.C.; and Cody culture of about 6500 B.C.), were descendants of the Big Game Hunters or new arrivals to the Southwest. Currently, a gap in the archeological record of around 500 years exists, so it is not clear whether the Big Game Hunters moved on to the Great Plains or other regions, developed into arid-land dwellers, or were replaced by an entirely new group of people. What is known is that the new arid-land dwellers were forced to rely on a more varied diet. An absence of larger

Preceding pages: Anasazi ruins of Pueblo Bonito, Chaco Culture National Historical Park, at sunset.
PHOTO BY JACK DYKINGA

Left: Oak Tree House, Mesa Verde National Park, southwestern Colorado. Anasazi Basketmaker III (Modified Basket Maker) pithouse remains dating between A.D. 575 and 800 have been discovered at Mesa Verde along with mesa top pueblo villages that began to be constructed around A.D. 800. Cliff dwellings were built during the thirteenth century. Mesa Verde contains more than 4,000 prehistoric sites.
PHOTO BY GEORGE H. H. HUEY

Right: Navajo hogan at Canyon de Chelly National Monument. After abandonment by the Anasazi, Canyon de Chelly has been utilized in historic times by both the Navajo and the Hopi.
PHOTO BY TOM TILL

mammals resulted in the hunting of smaller animals and gathering of nuts, roots, grains, and berries to supplement their diets. Recovered tools, including a variety of scrapers, knives and projectile points, show them to have been unspecialized hunters and gatherers.

Changing to a diet that included more plant life necessitated new levels of resourcefulness and ingenuity. Seeds needed to be finely ground to be digested. Grinding stones were developed with the bottom stone hollowed out to contain the grain and the top stone shaped to fit the hand as it was rolled over seeds until they became reduced to a powder. Beaters, trays and baskets were made to collect, carry and store food. Waterproofing with resins and gums was introduced to store water and allow the cooking of grains into gruel and flat cakes. During this development stage, Southwestern cultures, still nomadic, wandered the region in pursuit of game and plant species.

The adoption of agriculture, perhaps as early as 3000 B.C., with plantings of corn, beans, squash and melons, set the stage for establishing permanent villages. Crops were planted, using digging sticks to make holes for seeds which, when planted, were left to nature for water and nourishment as planters continued to forage for plants and game. It was now necessary for the tribe to return to the area to harvest ripened crops, giving rise to villages inhabited on a seasonal basis.

Even as agriculture played an increased role in the sustenance of Southwestern tribes, it was slow to change the way of life of those who domesticated the crops. Evidence of wells dug to provide water in dry areas has been found dating to this period near Clovis, New Mexico, and it is assumed they existed in other areas as well. Hunting and gathering were still essential for survival. It was not until around 300 B.C. that irrigation on a substantial scale appeared in villages along the Gila and Salt rivers in Arizona, revealing increased reliance on agriculture as a major part of subsistence. This consequently paved the way for development of year-round villages.

By A.D. 500, there were few permanently occupied Southwestern villages, as most tribes were still at least semi-nomadic, returning to base camps to plant and harvest crops while

continuing to gather wild plant foods and hunt game to supplement their existence.

There were three major Indian cultures in the prehistoric Southwest: the Hohokam, a desert agricultural group; the Mogollon, hunters and gatherers in the mountain regions; and the Anasazi, cliff dwellers in northern areas of the Southwest during the later stage of their development. Other important groups included the Sinagua, who lived near Flagstaff and in the Verde Valley area, and the Salado, who lived in the Tonto Basin and mountains near Globe and Miami in east-central Arizona.

Major Southwestern Indian tribes of historic times are related in part to the prehistoric Pueblo cultures, Plains Indians, and Athabascan tribes from Canada. Tribes of historic times include the Acoma, Apache, Caddo, Chemehuevi, Cochiti, Cocopah, Comanche, Havasupai, Hopi, Hualapai, Isleta, Jemez, Kiowa, Laguna, Mohave, Maricopa, Nambre, Navajo, Paiute, Picuris, Pima, Pojaque, San Felipe, San Ildefonso, San Juan, Sandia, Santa Ana, Santa Clara, Santo Domingo, Taos, Tesque, Tohono O'otam, Ute, Yavapai, Yaqui, Yuma, Zia, and Zuñi.

The first Europeans to encounter Southwestern Indian tribes were Spanish explorers in the 1540's who found the region of little economic interest. Franciscan and Jesuit missionaries were responsible for much of the Spanish colonization of the region, although they met great resistance from the Indians, who had little use for a new God. The Spaniards failed to gain a significant foothold in the Southwest.

Uneasy relations with the Indians kept them contained to small areas, subject to continual raiding by hostile tribes restricted the growth of their settlements.

The Americans entered the Southwest after the Mexican War of 1846 and were successful in subduing the Indians. The superior weapons and forces of the Americans were brought against the last raiding bands of Comanches, Apaches, Utes, Navajos and other tribes that had successfully resisted Spanish colonization. By the late 1800's, the Indians of the Southwest were relegated to life on the reservations.

Below: Betatakin, an Anasazi ruin protected in an alcove measuring 452 feet high, 370 feet wide and 135 feet deep. Navajo National Monument.
PHOTO BY JEFF GNASS

ANCIENT INHABITANTS

The first human inhabitants of the Southwest were Paleo-Indian nomads who roamed the region in pursuit of large prehistoric animals including mastodons, mammoths, camels and elephants. As prehistoric mammals became extinct, the big-game hunters were replaced by Archaic cultures who hunted smaller game and gathered wild foods for their sustenance. The introduction of agriculture from groups in the south paved the way for the development of permanent villages.

The earliest inhabitants of the Southwest were descendants of *Homo sapiens* who migrated from Asia via an ancient land bridge across the Bering Strait during the Pleistocene Epoch, or Ice Age, at least 37,000 years ago. At this time, nearly one-sixth of the world's surface was covered with ice. The formation of massive glaciers caused the oceans to recede and in some places sea level was lowered as much as 300 feet, exposing a 56 mile strip of the ocean's floor between northeastern Siberia and northwestern Alaska. The exposed land allowed grazing animals and early hunters access to the New World.

These early hunters were true men who walked erect, possessed fire, wore clothing of fur and skin, and used tools made of flint and bone. Their greatest concentrations of fire sites and artifacts have been found on the limestone plateaus of Texas, where the oldest remains of man in the New World have been discovered. Radiocarbon testing has proven that remains of burnt wood from one campsite found in the region date beyond the range of the carbon-14 technique, which can establish dates as far back as 37,000 years ago.

Archeologists named these early hunters the Texas Paleo-Americans and were surprised to discover that they had massive teeth, longer heads than any race of modern man, and leg bones that were flat and curved. They were quite unlike the later Paleo-Indians or prehistoric American Indians who were previously thought to have been the earliest inhabitants of the New World. It is thought they were a Caucasoid race that originated in Central Asia.

Like all people of the Ice Age, these ancient people pursued herds of elephants, mastodons, mammoths, giant sloths, camels, horses and prehistoric bison (approximately twice the size and perhaps four times the weight of those found in recorded history). It is believed they led their nomadic existence in the New World for several thousand years before disappearing from the archeological record. It is currently unknown whether their race died out entirely or changed so much over the following millennia that they were no longer recognizable. What is known is that the next Southwestern inhabitants discovered by archeologists, also big game hunters, were distinctly Asian and bore no resemblance to the earlier inhabitants.

The first of these early Asian nomadic tribes to reach the regions of the Southwest, more than 12,000 years ago, are known as the Big Game Hunters or the Elephant Hunters. These early nomads found the region quite different than it is today. Climactic conditions were far more tropical: a juniper savanna covered the arid desert surrounding Las Vegas, Nevada; an open savanna of pine and spruce, dotted with shallow lakes, filled the now treeless plains of the Llano Estacado in eastern New Mexico and Texas; and Late Pleistocene streams flowed throughout the Southwest. This environment provided habitat for mastodons, mammoths, elephants, horses, camels, antelope, bison, sloth, tapir, peccary, deer and rabbit– as well as for hunters who preyed on them for survival.

Paleo-Indian hunters depended on hunting the larger prehistoric beasts. Using organized teamwork to kill their prey, these Paleo-Indian

Left: Unexcavated ruin of Yapashi Pueblo, circa A.D. 1200 to 1400, Bandelier National Monument. To an untrained eye many important archeological sites can be easy to overlook. It was not until this century that archeologists began to give proper care to determining relationships of objects unearthed by comparing their stratigraphic location.
PHOTO BY GEORGE H.H. HUEY

Right: A row of painted Anasazi handprints on a wall of White Canyon, Natural Bridges National Monument, Utah. Indian artists painted, or carved, drawings on rock surfaces. Petroglyphs were made by scratching designs on a rock surface. Drawings created by painting are called pictographs.
PHOTO BY TOM DANIELSEN

hunters fashioned spearheads of stone with detachable foreshafts. When the shaft became detached after entering the prey, the animals could not easily work the embedded point from wounds, which hastened their death.

The exact arrival of Paleo-Indian inhabitants in the region is still unknown. Conservative archeologists currently place the date between 10,000-12,000 B.C. Archeologists during this century have been able to establish evidence to support early man's presence in the region. In 1927, J. D. Figgins discovered man-made artifacts in association with extinct mammals at the Folsom site in New Mexico, that have been dated at around 9000 B.C. The Folsom site was discovered by a cowboy, George McJunkin, in the 1920's. In 1928, Byron C. Cummings uncovered a similar find at the Double Adobe site in southeastern Arizona.

Two kill sites, excavated by archeologists from the University of Arizona in the 1950's, were discovered in Arizona and have been dated approximately 11,000 years ago. At the first, along the banks of Greenbush Creek near Naco in southeastern Arizona, an extinct mammoth was excavated. Archeologists found eight stone spearheads in the skeletal remains of the body portion of the 13 foot-tall animal. A second site, along the San Pedro River on Lehner Ranch, unearthed the bones of nine elephants along with a primitive horse, a bison, and a tapir. Ashes from two fires in the vicinity, probably made to roast meat from the kill, have been carbon dated to place the event near 9000 B.C.

The early Big Game Hunters harvested most of their needs from the mammals they hunted.

PROJECTILE POINTS

Prehistoric Indians of the Southwest all relied on some form of projectile point, or tip, to help penetrate prey. A projectile point was affixed to spear shafts in the earliest cultures. The atlatl, a rigid board around two feet long with a notch near the top in which spear, dart or arrow shafts were inserted, was used from about 10,000 B.C. until the first centuries A.D. when it was replaced by the more accurate and powerful bow and arrow.

Projectile points found at Homolovi Ruins.
PHOTO BY MICHAEL COLLIER

Projectile points are named for the location where they are first discovered and are used to identify different cultures by refinements in design of the points, such as the appearance of longitudinal grooves to allow blood to flow freely from wounds. Prehistoric Southwestern projectile points have been found made of obsidian, rhyolite, jasper, calcite and other rocks and minerals.

After a group of men would kill an animal, usually from ambush near a watering hole, women would use stone knives to strip the animal's hide from its carcass, using stone scrapers to remove fat and flesh, a process that helped preserve and shape the hide which was then fashioned into clothing, robes and other items.

Archeologists have now developed many theories about earlier cultures based on the remnants of their tool kits. Refinements in design of projectile points, such as the first appearance of longitudinal grooves on both faces of a spearhead (so blood could flow more freely from a wound), helps to distinguish one culture from another. Archeologists name projectile points for the location they are first discovered. Sandia, Clovis and Folsom points are named for New Mexico sites. A projectile point may first be discovered in one area, but it is never certain whether that particular area was its point of origin or if it was obtained through trade, captured in war, or acquired by other means.

As the polar ice caps melted, the Southwest's climate became increasingly drier between 8000 and 7000 B.C., causing a decrease in annual rainfall of three to four inches and an increase in mean annual temperature between three and four degrees. Lush vegetation the larger mammals depended on for survival became increasingly scarce, as did the animals themselves. Final extinction of mammoths, mastodons, camels, elephants, horses and other large species may have been hastened by the Big Game Hunters themselves as they struggled to find the last of the diminishing herds to support their bands. Consequently, the Big Game Hunters themselves disappeared.

It is uncertain whether the next inhabitants to appear, Paleo-Indians (evidenced by discovery of complexes including the Clovis culture, dating earlier than 9000 B.C.; Folsom culture, slightly after 9000 B.C.; Agate Basin culture around 8000 B.C.; and Cody culture of about 6500 B.C.), were descendants of the Big Game Hunters or new arrivals to the Southwest.

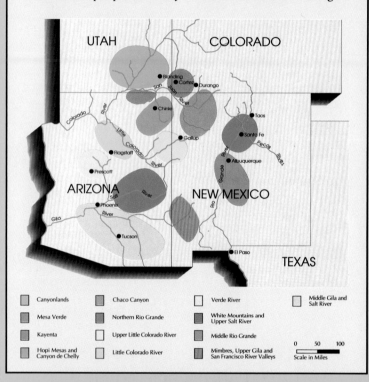

CONCENTRATIONS OF PREHISTORIC INDIAN RUINS

The Southwest plays an important role in preserving artifacts of the earliest inhabitants of the New World. The Southwest's semi-arid climate has helped preserve many artifacts that could not have survived in regions with a wetter climate. The map below shows areas with the greatest concentrations of aboriginal artifacts to be found in the region.

	Canyonlands		Chaco Canyon		Verde River		Middle Gila and Salt River
	Mesa Verde		Northern Rio Grande		White Mountains and Upper Salt River		
	Kayenta		Upper Little Colorado River		Middle Rio Grande		
	Hopi Mesas and Canyon de Chelly		Little Colorado River		Mimbres, Upper Gila and San Francisco River Valleys		

0   50   100
Scale in Miles

Currently, a gap in the archeological record of around 500 years exists, so it is unclear whether the Big Game Hunters moved on to the Great Plains or other regions, developed into arid-land dwellers, or were replaced by an entirely new group of people. What is known is that these new arid-land dwellers were forced to rely on a more varied diet.

Clovis finds have been reported over the entire Southwest and much of the Great Basin. Folsom complexes have been found east of the Arizona-New Mexico border. Remains of the Agate Basin complex occur in central and eastern New Mexico and the Cody complex is widely spread over the eastern and northern Southwest. At present, there is no evidence of a direct relation between these cultures and the earlier Big Game Hunters.

Early Archaic cultures, often characterized as belonging to the widespread Desert Culture, include four distinct groups: the Western, or San Dieguito-Pinto, who inhabited western Arizona and southern Nevada; the Southern, or Cochise tradition, found in the southeastern and east-central regions of Arizona and New Mexico's southwestern and west-central areas; the Northern, or Oshara tradition, of northern Arizona, southeastern Utah, southwestern Colorado, and northwestern New Mexico; and the Southeastern tradition, represented by the Fresnal and Hueco related complexes.

The last areas of the Southwest abandoned by the Big Game Hunters of the Cody complex, around 6000 B.C., were the northeastern and southeastern regions. The San Dieguito-Pinto were then established in the west and the Cochise people were inhabiting the south. After environmental changes caused the last of the large mammal hunters to leave the region, the Oshara tradition began to appear.

Cultural remains of the San Dieguito-Pinto tradition are thought to date from around 7000 B.C. until sometime after 5000 B.C., and resemble those of the earlier Clovis culture found to the east. Recovered tools, including a variety of scrapers, knives and projectile points, show them to have been unspecialized hunters and gatherers.

The Cochise culture, named for artifacts found along creek banks in Cochise County, Arizona, appeared at their earliest sites, called the Sulpher Springs phase, between 7000 B.C. and 6000 B.C. The Cochise were forced to adjust to an environment with fewer resources. An absence of the larger mammals resulted in the hunting of smaller animals and the gathering of nuts, roots, grains, and berries to supplement their simple diets.

The Oshara tradition is representative of the northern Southwest between 5500 B.C. and A.D. 400. Early Archaic materials recovered belonging to the Oshara tradition date between 5500 and 4800 B.C. Tool kits and settlement patterns differ so greatly that no connection with the earlier Cody complex or other Paleo-Indians is clearly evident. Deer and bighorn sheep were the larger game animals and the people were now gatherers as well as hunters. Seeds, berries, nuts, roots, and other plant parts were collected and small game such as rodents, rabbits, birds and squirrels were killed with spear and dart throwers, called atlatls, or trapped with snares. Even insects and reptiles became part of people's diets.

Changing to a diet that included more plants necessitated new levels of resourcefulness and ingenuity. Seeds needed to be finely ground to be digested. Grinding stones were developed with the bottom stone hollowed out to contain the grain and the top stone shaped to fit the hand as it was rolled over seeds until they became reduced to a powder. Beaters, trays and baskets were made to collect, carry and store food. Waterproofing with resins and gums was introduced to store water and allow the cooking of grains into gruel and flat cakes. During this development stage, Southwestern

cultures, still nomadic, wandered the region in pursuit of game and plant species.

The adoption of agriculture, perhaps as early as 3000 B.C., with plantings of corn, beans, squash and melons, set the stage for establish-

Above: Split-twig figurines made by Desert Archaic people. These willow figurines were found in a cave site in Grand Canyon National Park and are between 3,000 and 4,000 years old. The figures are thought to have been used to ensure good hunting.
PHOTO BY TOM BEAN

ing permanent villages. Crops were planted, using digging sticks to make holes for seeds which, when planted, were left to nature for water and nourishment as the planters continued to forage for wild plants and game. It was now necessary for the tribe to return to the area to harvest ripened crops, forming the basis for villages inhabited on a seasonal basis.

Even as agriculture played an increased role in the overall sustenance of Southwestern tribes, it was slow to change the way of life of those who domesticated the crops. Evidence of wells dug to provide water in dry areas has been found dating to this period near Clovis, New Mexico, and it is assumed wells existed in other locations as well. Hunting and gathering were still essential for survival. It was not until around 300 B.C. that irrigation on a substantial scale appeared in villages along the Gila and Salt rivers of Arizona, revealing an increased reliance on agriculture as a major part of subsistence. This

consequently paved the way for development of the first year-round villages.

Snaketown, on the north bank of the Gila River in Arizona, was a year-round village inhabited by the Hohokam from around 300 B.C. (although some put this date as late as A.D. 500) until A.D 1000. More than 200 rooms have been excavated and research shows that Snaketown's inhabitants relied heavily on production of domesticated crops and had developed skillful irrigation techniques.

By A.D. 500, there were few permanently occupied Southwestern villages, as most tribes were still at least semi-nomadic, returning to base camps to plant and harvest crops while continuing to gather wild plant foods and hunt game to supplement their existence. The stage was being set, however, for the rise of cultures whose remains we find in abundance today.

There were three major Indian cultures in the prehistoric Southwest: the Hohokam, a desert agricultural group; the Mogollon, hunters and gatherers in the mountain regions; and the Anasazi, cliff dwellers in later stages in northern areas of the Southwest. Other important groups included the Sinagua, who lived near Flagstaff and in the Verde Valley area, and the Salado, who lived in the Tonto Basin and mountains near Globe and Miami in east-central Arizona.

MAJOR PREHISTORIC INDIAN CULTURES

The three major Indian cultures in the prehistoric Southwest were the Hohokam, who lived in river valleys in the southern desert and were an agricultural group; the Mogollon, who were hunter-gatherers; and the Anasazi, who were cliff dwellers. The Sinagua lived near Flagstaff and the Verde Valley and comprised traits from all three major cultures. The Salado lived in east-central Arizona and are thought to be a blend of two or more major cultures.

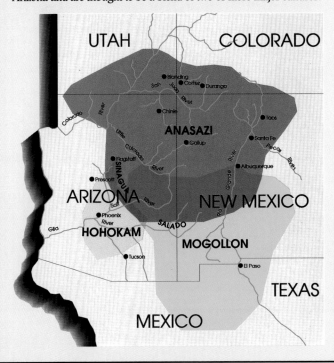

Ancient Indian cultures of the Southwest are often identified and named for the location where their first relics are discovered. Individual cultures developed at different rates and can often be recognized by the elements found in their tool kits. There is evidence showing different groups came into contact with one another, or at least with elements created by other cultures, either through trade, capture through warfare, or by chance. Indians would adapt ideas and designs for tools and other items they admired. This, at times, can be somewhat confusing to archeologists, who normally assign the introduction of a new style to the culture where they first discover new styles of tools.

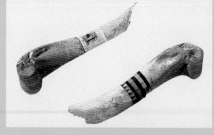

Above: Inlaid bone scrapers made of deer bone. Chaco Culture National Historical Park. PHOTO BY GEORGE H. H. HUEY

The earliest tools were fashioned from sticks, stones, and minerals such as obsidian, rhyolite, jasper and calcite. Projectile points, scrapers, flakers, knives and other tools were shaped by hard stones into useful shapes and used to collect, process and prepare food, and to make clothing and shelter. Sticks were used as spear shafts and as digging tools. Sticks and stones were joined together to make spears with sharpened stone projectile points. The introduction of agriculture, at a later date, brought stone heads to the ends of sticks. These were primitive hoes that greatly increased the efficiency of digging sticks. Stone was also used by early cultures as vessels to store food items and stones were often fashioned into metates and manos to grind corn and seeds.

Adaptation of agriculture brought the settlement of permanent villages and the construction of permanent homes. Stone axes (rocks tied to sticks) were used to cut timbers for beams and rafters, and to shape poles for posts and ladders. Stone was fashioned into hafted saws and used to hammer and chisel rocks used in masonry

Above: Anasazi stone axe. Aztec Ruins National Monument. PHOTO BY GEORGE H. H. HUEY

construction. Grooved stones were used to shape spears, darts and arrow shafts. Even early combs and other personal items were made of sticks and stones.

Although stone was normally used to make tools including axes, hammers, projectile points, knives and scrapers, small tools were also fashioned from other materials. Bone scrapers, needles and awls were commonly made from deer leg bones that were ground on rocks to achieve sharp points, although some bone awls were also made from turkey and other small animal bone. Splintered bones were shaped to a fine point to make needles, awls and other small tools that were used to pierce hides and sew. Bones of birds, which are hollow, were utilized to make tubes and whistles.

Bone tools were also helpful in basketmaking and weaving. Woven fibers were fashioned from reeds, grasses

THE EVOLUTION OF POTTERY SHAPES

Prior to the introduction of pottery, gourds served a variety of uses as vessels for carrying and storing food and water, and as utensils for serving and eating. The earliest pottery forms were copied from the natural shapes of gourds. Fuller gourd shapes were utilized as jars and pitchers, while partial gourd shapes were the inspiration for bowls and plates. Pottery shapes copied from vertical portions of the gourd became the first serving utensils– early ladles and handled bowls.

Before pottery appeared in the Southwest, baskets were used in the preparation of cooked foods; heated stones were placed inside the baskets to warm the food. The introduction of pottery was one of the most important changes in the lives of early Indian cultures. Pottery allowed for greatly improved cooking techniques and increased the variety of foods in peoples' diets. Preservation of stored foods was also greatly improved.

Early pottery was made from pure clay, which was useless when it dried. Grass and straw were used to temper the clay but would easily burn when placed on a fire. Finally, sand and grit were used successfully to temper pottery and produce wares that remained strong and serviceable after they were baked.

Each distinct group of early Indian inhabitants developed their own styles of pottery. This helps archeologists identify them. As a group's pottery making skills improved, wares that were once plain and not decorated would begin to exhibit painted designs and other embellishments. Different styles can be used to identify develop-

Gourd

Full gourd-shaped jar

Small mouthed jar

Pot (incurved jar)

Jar   True Bowl   Shallow Bowl   Plate

Half-gourd ladle

Half-gourd copied in clay.

Handle and bowl becoming separated.

Handle and bowl separated. Grooved handle disappearing.

True bowl-and-handle ladle.

ment stages of individual groups. The careful management of ruins is necessary to uncover pottery properly. Cataloging the comparative relationship of pottery to other relics unearthed can provide valuable insight into the inhabitants of an area. Much of what we have learned about the sequence of the development of individual prehistoric Indian cultures has been determined through studying their pottery.

and other fibers to store and transport food, and, when lined with pitch, to hold water. Yucca fibers were utilized to make burden straps for carrying baskets, sandals and other items. Although the introduction of basket-making was an important event in the development of the Indian cultures, and baskets are still utilized by people of all cultures, the baskets have certain limitations.

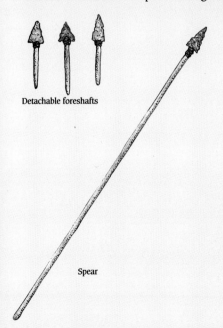

Above: Yucca fiber sandal. Aztec Ruins National Park, New Mexico.
PHOTO BY GEORGE H. H. HUEY

Food storage in baskets was not air-tight for preserving surplus items for future use. Cooking food in baskets, which was accomplished by placing heated stones in the baskets with the food, destroyed the baskets and did not fully cook the food; this limited the types of foods found in early cultures' diets.

Prior to the introduction of pottery, gourds were used for carrying and storing food and water, and as utensils for serving and eating. Early pottery forms were copied from shapes of the gourds. Fuller gourd shapes were copied for jars and pitchers, while partial gourd shapes inspired bowls and plates. Shapes copied from vertical portions of the gourd were the design for early ladles and handled bowls used as serving utensils.

Pottery allowed for greatly improved cooking techniques and increased the variety of foods consumed because preservation of stored foods

Above: Pottery, dating between A.D. 1100 and 1150, found at the Walhalla Glades site. Grand Canyon National Park, Arizona.
PHOTO BY GEORGE H. H. HUEY

was greatly improved.

Each group of early Southwestern Indian inhabitants developed their own distinct styles of pottery and tools, incorporating shapes and materials that help archeologists to identify them. As the skill levels of the Southwestern Indian cultures improved, early forms of pottery that were plain and undecorated began to exhibit painted designs and other embellishments. Tool kits that were crude became more refined. The different styles can be used to identify development stages of individual groups. The careful management of ruins is necessary to recover relics from prehistoric sites. The cataloging of comparative relationships of pottery and other unearthed relics often provides

Above: Chaco Culture jet frog with turquoise inlay.
PHOTO BY GEORGE H. H. HUEY

valuable insight into the inhabitants of an area. Much of what we have learned about the sequence of the development of individual prehistoric Indian cultures has been learned through studying pottery and other relics.

Not all objects made by prehistoric cultures were developed as tools and household utensils. Jewelry was fashioned as ornaments from a variety of materials including bone, shell, rock, feather and minerals, often combining several elements in one piece. Game pieces were made from bone and rock. Fetishes, thought to give supernatural powers to their owners, were made from stone, shell, antler and other materials.

THE EVOLUTION OF WEAPONS

The earliest prehistoric Indian weapons were stones and sticks. At first sticks were simply sharpened on one end to allow easier penetration, becoming a spear. Later, projectile points of stone or minerals were attached to spears which greatly increased their effectiveness. Detachable foreshafts were introduced allowing projectile points to remain in prey after the spear was removed, hastening the animal's death. Refinements in design of projectile points, such as the appearance of longitudinal grooves on faces of spearheads so blood could flow more freely from a wound, further increased the spear's effectiveness.

More than 10,000 years ago, the atlatl, or spear thrower was in widespread use in the Southwest. The atlatl, a short rigid stick with a groove on one end to place darts or spears, extended the thrower's arm, which increased the force of the dart or spear by about 60 percent.

Atlatls remained in use until the bow and arrow, a far superior and more accurate weapon, was introduced in the Southwest somewhere around A.D. 500. The bow and arrow quickly relaced the spear throwers.

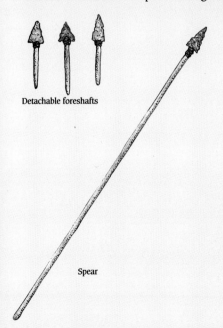

Detachable foreshafts

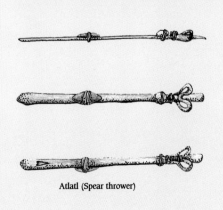

Spear

Atlatl (Spear thrower)

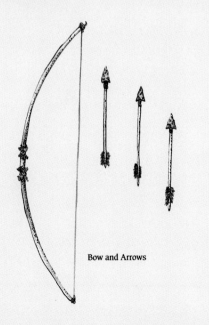

Bow and Arrows

THE HOHOKAM

The Hohokam produced excellent pottery and clay figurines. Their stone tools, vessels, and art objects were also well made, as was their work with shells, which they used to fashion ornaments and mosaics of exceptional beauty. Designs were drawn on the shell with pitch; the shell was then soaked in an acidic solution–probably fermented from saguaro cactus fruit; the unprotected shell surface was etched by the acid, leaving the pitch-protected design raised. This process preceded European metal etching by hundreds of years. Hohokam shellwork has been found at Anasazi, Mogollon, and Sinagua sites.

Named from the Tohono O'odham/Pima word for "those who have vanished," or more accurately, "all used up," the Hohokam were desert farmers who lived in scattered villages in the Sonoran Desert of central and southern Arizona for more than a millennia. They were the first Southwestern farmers to use irrigation, digging gravity-fed canals along the Gila and Salt rivers. More than 300 miles of canals have been discovered in the Salt River Valley alone that were built by the Hohokam, the largest prehistoric system found in North America.

The Hohokam used irrigation to raise corn (maize), beans, barley, cotton, tobacco, squash, agave and other crops, allowing them to devote less time to foraging, although they harvested pads of prickly pear cactus, saguaro fruit and mesquite beans to supplement their fare. This agricultural existence resulted in settlements and permanent villages located near the crops.

Some scholars place the Hohokam's arrival in the region at around 300 B.C. while others believe their arrival could be as late as A.D. 500. Debate over their origins also exists, with some archeologists believing they migrated from Mexico and others feeling the Hohokam and the Mogollon were descendants of the Cochise people. Most do agree to four major periods of Hohokam culture: Pioneer period–300 B.C. to A.D. 550 (some believe A.D. 300-500 is a more accurate arrival); Colonial period–A.D. 550 to 900; Sedentary period–A.D. 900 to 1100; and Classic period–A.D. 1100 to 1450.

During the Pioneer period the Hohokam lived in houses built in pits in the ground of mud and stick enclosed with clay. During the Colonial period true pithouses appeared with upright poles supporting roofs of reeds, grass and mud built over the pit. Increased trade and social interaction with Mexico was evident. Mesoamerican style ball courts, possibly used for semi-sacred games or at least as a center of community activity, began to appear.

During the Classic period major changes in architecture appear. Walled villages with multistory above-ground adobe buildings appeared along with platform mounds, filled with trash, earth and covered with plaster, whose exact uses are still unknown.

The Hohokam produced excellent pottery and clay figurines. Their stone tools, vessels, and art objects were also well made, as was their work with shells, mostly from the Gulf of California, which they used to fashion ornaments and mosaics of exceptional beauty. Designs were drawn on the shell with pitch; the shell was then soaked in an acidic solution–probably juice fermented from saguaro cactus fruit; the unprotected shell surface was etched by the acid, leaving the pitch-protected design raised. This process preceded European metal etching by hundreds of years. Hohokam shellwork has been found at Anasazi, Mogollon, and Sinagua sites, most probably acquired by trade.

During the fifteenth century the Hohokam abandoned their desert villages. Controversy exists between those who believe Tohono O'odham (Papago), Pima and other Southwestern groups are descendants of the Hohokam and those who believe they replaced the Hohokam who had moved completely out of the region.

Left: Casa Grande Ruin. In 1694, Father Eusebio Francisco Kino, a Jesuit missionary, was the first European to visit Casa Grande. The four story tower, the largest existing Hohokam structure, served as a landmark for early Spanish travelers. The tower's function is undetermined, although it may have been an astronomical observatory. In 1932, the National Park Service built the roof over the ruin to prevent its further erosion. Casa Grande Ruins National Monument.
PHOTO BY TOM DANIELSEN

Right: Fortaleza (fortified hill) is an ancient fortified Hohokam village overlooking the Gila River near Gila Bend, Arizona. The Hohokam were the first Southwestern farmers to use irrigation, digging gravity-fed canals along the Gila and Salt rivers. More than 300 miles of canals, the largest prehistoric system found in North America, have been discovered in the Salt River Valley alone that were built by the Hohokam.
PHOTO BY TOM DANIELSEN

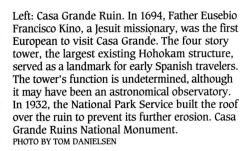

THE MOGOLLON

Early Mogollon pithouses were round or irregular in shape, built partially underground with wooden beams to support the roof structure, and ramped or stepped entrances. Large communal rooms, around 300 to more than 1,000 square feet, were a central part of village life. From about A.D. 600 to 900, Mogollon pithouses were mostly rectangular and were more carefully constructed than earlier structures. During this period, the Mogollon moved from their earlier high ground into valleys closer to their fields. After A.D. 900, the Mogollon began to construct above ground dwellings of masonry construction.

Primarily hunters and gatherers in the mountainous regions of southeastern Arizona and southwestern New Mexico, the Mogollon culture was named for the Mogollon Mountains of New Mexico by early archeologists who did not want to link their culture with living Native American groups. When many Mogollon sites were excavated prior to 1920, archeologists thought them to be regional variations of the Anasazi (Hisatsinom) culture. By the first Pecos Conference in 1927, archeologists had begun to recognize several cultures in the Southwest instead of one culture with regional variations. In the early 1930's, H.S. Gladwin and Emil W. Haury were the first archeologists to recognize the Mogollon as a culture distinct from the Hohokam of southern Arizona deserts and the Anasazi of the Colorado Plateau to the north.

The Mogollon are generally considered to be descendants of the earlier Cochise culture, whose earliest presence in the region dates to around 6000-5000 B.C. The Mogollon culture began to appear around 300-200 B.C. and, like their Cochise ancestors, settled in areas where the animals they hunted, deer, pronghorn, bison, rabbit, turkey and mountain sheep, were plentiful. The Cochise people were the first Southwestern culture to cultivate corn, and are thought to have passed this skill along to the Mogollon, who also grew small amounts of beans and squash, although they relied less on agriculture and more on hunting and gathering than neighboring Hohokam or Anasazi cultures. The Mogollon gathered wild foods including walnuts, prickly pear cactus,

acorns, pinyon nuts, agave, tansy mustard, sunflower seeds and wild tomato. Agriculture became a more important source of sustenance for the Mogollon around A.D. 700, as they began planting improved strains of corn along with squash, beans and cotton.

The Mogollon were among the first Indian cultures of the Southwest to make pottery for storing food and water. Their earliest examples were a plain brown ware, called Alma Plain, and a polished red ware called San Francisco Red that appeared around A.D. 200. A red-on-brown painted type, Mogollon Red-on-brown, appeared about A.D. 300. Around A.D. 750, the Mogollon potters introduced a painted red-on-white ware called Three Circle Red-on-white, which marked a startling change in design that was popular and widely produced until about A.D. 900, when the red-on-brown and red-on-white were completely replaced by black-on-white designs that are thought to have been inspired by the Anasazi. The black-on-white styles evolved into the Mimbres Classic Black-on-white that the Mogollon produced until about A.D. 1200 and have since become famous for. The popularity and value of these wares, when first discovered, caused widespread looting of Mogollon ruins that devastated many important archeological sites.

The early Mogollon lived in small villages, normally less than fifty dwellings, that were built on mountain ridges and high mesas. The buildings were of pithouse construction, round or irregular in shape, partially underground with wood beams supporting the roof structure, and with ramped or stepped entrances that

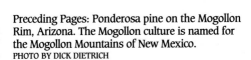

Preceding Pages: Ponderosa pine on the Mogollon Rim, Arizona. The Mogollon culture is named for the Mogollon Mountains of New Mexico.
PHOTO BY DICK DIETRICH

Left: Kinishba Pueblo contains the remains of two large Mogollon culture structures of about 200 rooms each. Kinishba was occupied from around A.D. 1250 to 1325. Kinishba Ruin is located on the Fort Apache Indian Reservation in Arizona.
PHOTO BY JERRY JACKA

Right: Mogollon culture cliff dwellings in Gila Cliff Dwellings National Monument, New Mexico. These structures were built around A.D. 1270 and were abandoned by the early 1300's.
PHOTO BY GEORGE H.H. HUEY

normally faced east or southeast. A large communal room, ranging from around 300 to more than 1,000 square feet, was a central part of village life. Lack of everyday living items, or burial remains of the dead beneath the floors, in excavations of these communal rooms suggest that they were used for special purposes. Although it cannot be said for certain they were used for ceremonies uses, some contained artifacts that may point to religious use.

From A.D. 600 to 900, Mogollon pithouses were mostly rectangular and more carefully constructed than earlier structures. During this period, the Mogollon moved from their earlier high ground into valleys that placed them closer to their fields. Anasazi influences began to show in their pottery and architecture.

About A.D. 900, the Mogollon began building their first surface pueblos. These structures were above ground and were of stone masonry construction. Mogollon pueblos ranged from as few as 4 or 5 rooms to the 500 room Grasshopper Pueblo in the White Mountains of Arizona that was built between A.D. 1275 and A.D. 1300.

The Mogollon are not thought to have been

Right: Cliff dwellings in a natural cave. The room walls were made of rock (Gila Conglomerate) by the Mogollon between A.D. 1280 and the early 1300's. Gila Cliff Dwellings National Monument is in New Mexico.
PHOTO BY TOM DANIELSEN

a particularly inventive people. Most tools that have been uncovered at their ruins tend to be quite primitive. Many archeologists feel that advances in architecture and ceramic pottery by the Mogollon around A.D. 1000 were the result of the Anasazi moving into Mogollon territory, and that the only true Mogollon were the earlier pithouse builders. Others feel there was contact between the two cultures, and that the Anasazi influenced the Mogollon, but did not entirely replace them.

Mogollon sites from earlier periods are poorly preserved. Later developments, including the Gila Cliff Dwellings in New Mexico and the Kinishba Pueblo, with two large structures (each with around 200 rooms), in the White Mountains of Arizona, are among the best preserved Mogollon sites. Kinishba was occupied around A.D. 1250 to 1325 and contains traces of the Mogollon and Anasazi cultures.

Above: Mogollon culture bird pictographs. In the early 1930's, archeologists H.S. Gladwin and Emil W. Haury were the first to recognize the Mogollon as a culture distinct from the Hohokam of southern Arizona deserts and the Anasazi of the Colorado Plateau to the north.
PHOTO BY GEORGE H. H. HUEY

Gila Cliff Dwellings National Monument also shows elements of both Mogollon and Anasazi cultures. About A.D. 1270, the Mogollon moved to the cliffs above Cliff Dweller Canyon, for reasons that are currently not completely understood but possibly include: a depletion of natural resources in, or overpopulation of, their former homelands; increased raiding by other Indian groups; or possibly there was infighting among themselves. At Gila Cliff Dwellings the Mogollon built masonry structures in a series of caves, high above the canyon floor, some of which are connected. These dwellings were occupied for only a short period of time and abandoned by the early 1300's. Although no one is exactly sure why Gila Cliff sites were abandoned, it is possible that the Anasazi had

Below: Summer thunderstorm over Crescent Lake in Arizona's White Mountains.
PHOTO BY LARRY ULRICH

completely absorbed this Mogollon group and they then may have left the area in search of more fertile farmlands.

One of the last pueblos to be occupied by the Mogollon was near Springerville, Arizona. Casa Malpais is a Spanish name meaning the "Badlands House." This 60-80 room pueblo was inhabited around A.D. 1265 to 1400. In 1990, archeologist John Hohmann examined Casa Malpais and discovered that fissures found in the caves, previously thought to have contained only trash, had been altered by their earlier inhabitants and contained about 3 to 4 acres of tunnels and chambers, some as wide as 50 feet and as much as 100 feet long.

These underground chambers were filled with human skeletal remains, unlike any site ever discovered north of Mexico. The State of Arizona gives some control over these remains to their likely descendants, in this case the Hopi and Zuni tribes, who now control access to these underground catacombs. No burial remains or burial objects are allowed to be removed from the site, nor

Above: San Francisco River valley, northwest of Silver City, New Mexico. The Mogollon culture occupied the valleys along the San Francisco and Mimbres rivers, lands that form a stark contrast with the otherwise arid region.
PHOTO BY MICHAEL COLLIER

will photography be allowed. This unique discovery will undoubtedly change much of what archeologists currently believe about the ceremonial aspects of the Mogollon.

Although Mogollon abandonment of their homelands by A.D. 1400 is still somewhat of a mystery, there are several theories regarding their dispersal. Below average rainfall may have affected their crops causing the Mogollon to relocate, warring factions may have entered the region, or they may have been completely absorbed by the Anasazi who then left in search of better farmlands.

Some scholars believe the Mogollon moved north into Zuni and Hopi country, which is a likely theory and is supported by both the Hopi and Zuni who claim the Mogollon as ancestors. Others believe they migrated to the Sierra Madre Mountains of Mexico where they became the Tarahumara Indians. It is probable that either one, or both, of these theories may be correct.

Right: Tonto Basin from the Mogollon Rim, Tonto National Forest, Arizona. The Upper Salt River, Tonto Basin and White Mountain areas of eastern Arizona contain important Mogollon sites, along with Anasazi and Hohokam sites, and the majority of Salado culture sites.
PHOTO BY LARRY ULRICH

THE EVOLUTION OF MOGOLLON POTTERY...

The Mogollon culture was among the first Southwest Indian groups to make pottery for storing food and water. The utilization of pottery for cooking allowed a more diverse and palatable fare than previous cooking methods which placed heated stones and food together in woven baskets. Pottery also proved much more durable than baskets against flames from the fire.

The earliest Mogollon pottery examples were a plain brown ware, known as Alma Plain, and a red ware called San Francisco Red that appeared around A.D. 200. Both styles were polished and unpainted. These plain wares were mainly jars and bowls that were continually produced throughout the entire Mogollon history.

Around A.D. 300 the painted Mogollon Red-on-brown ware began to appear, with broad red lines painted on a brown ware. After A.D. 750 Mogollon wares underwent a startling change to painted red-on-white wares known as Three Circle Red-on-white, which

Both Mimbres Bold Face and Mimbres Classic Black-on-white pottery were crafted by the Mogollon from A.D. 900 to 1200 and are some the finest examples of prehistoric pottery found in the Southwest.

remained popular and were produced until about A.D. 900, when the red-on-white and red-on-brown pottery styles were completely

Alma Plain and San Francisco Red appeared about A.D. 200.

Mogollon Red-on-brown ware began to appear by A.D. 300.

replaced by black-on-white wares that are thought to have been inspired by Anasazi designs. With the introduction of the black-on-white wares, the Mogollon added additional styles and shapes. Jars and bowls were joined by ladles, pitchers, and other vessels of various shapes and usages.

These black-and-white wares evolved into the Mimbres Bold Face and Mimbres Classic Black-on-white styles that were continually produced by the Mogollon until about A.D. 1200. These bold designs are known for their geometric styles which often depict animals, insects, birds, fish, and people, and include some very interesting combinations of different stylized creatures that are combined into one element.

Around A.D. 1100, polychrome pottery styles were developed by the Mogollon that included black and white designs painted on a red slipped background that were exquisite and are thought to have been produced mainly by the Mogollon, although at least some of these wares may have been trade items produced by other groups.

Of all Mogollon pottery, Mimbres Bold Face and Mimbres Black-on-white are considered to have been their crowning achievements. Both styles were crafted by the Mogollon from A.D. 900 to 1200 and are some the finest examples of prehistoric pottery found in the Southwest. These styles were so valued for their beauty when they were first discovered that widespread looting of ruins by pothunters, determined to obtain pottery for financial gain, devastated many important Mogollon archeological sites, destroying forever opportunities to learn more about the Mogollon.

After A.D. 750 painted red-on-white pottery known as Three Circle Red-on-white appeared.

THE ANASAZI

Archeologists are uncertain as to the origin of the Anasazi. Some believe they are descendants of the Desert Culture, while others feel they may have been a northern branch of the Mogollon. Most agree that they did not disappear from the Southwest and are ancestors of the present day Hopi and Zuni. The origin of the name Anasazi is a Navajo word meaning "enemy ancestors" or "ancient people who are not us" depending on the pronunciation. The Hopi have always claimed these earlier people as relatives and take offense to the term "Anasazi," preferring Hisatsinom, which literally means "people of long ago."

Thought to have been descendants of a branch of an Archaic Desert Culture who inhabited the Southwest from approximately 6000 B.C., or a branch of the Mogollon who wandered into the region from the south, the Anasazi are best known for cliff dwellings they inhabited during later years of their civilization. The Anasazi (Hisatsinom) first appeared around the birth of Christ in the Four Corners region of the Colorado Plateau. The ruins at Chaco Culture National Historical Park, Mesa Verde National Park and Canyon de Chelly National Monument, in addition to countless other sites scattered throughout the Colorado Plateau, are among the best preserved ruins found in North America and have attracted attention from around the world since their discovery in the late 1800's.

For the first 1,000 years of their civilization, however, the Anasazi did not construct the cliff dwellings they later became famous for; they lived instead in unprotected open-country communities. Their earlier dwellings, called pithouses, were structures built three to five feet in the ground with roofs supported by wooden poles and beams that were covered by brush and mud. The early Anasazi lived in small communities near the fields where they grew corn, squash and beans. They gathered wild foods including agave, walnuts, pinyon nuts, acorns, yucca, prickly pear, Indian ricegrass and wild potatoes; gathered other plants for use as medicines, fuel and building materials; and hunted game including elk, deer, pronghorn antelope, mountain sheep, rabbit, turkey, birds, fish and rodents. Archeologists believe, based on

this pattern of living in open country without the protection afforded by later cliff dwellings, that the Anasazi had relatively few, or perhaps no, natural enemies during these early years.

The various periods of the Anasazi culture have been defined by scientists as Basketmaker I, Basketmaker II, Basketmaker III, Pueblo I, Pueblo II, Pueblo III, Pueblo IV and Pueblo V. These earliest Anasazi (Hisatsinom) were the Basketmaker II who lived from about A.D. 1 to about A.D. 500. (The Basketmaker I designation refers to the earlier Archaic cultures believed by many archeologists to have been ancestors of the Anasazi.) Basketmaker II people grew crops of corn and squash, hunted with spears and spear throwers called atlatls, and gathered wild foods which they stored in baskets. At this stage the Anasazi had not developed pottery, so tightly woven baskets, some which were waterproofed on the inside with a coating of pitch, and small woven bags were used for storage. They lived in caves, rock shelters and in some areas built circular log houses with slightly depressed floors.

The Basketmaker III period, from around A.D. 500 to A.D. 700, represents a period of major change for the Anasazi: pottery was developed which proved much more practical for storing water and cooking hot foods; beans, which provided a good source of protein, were added to Anasazi crops; the more accurate bow and arrow replaced the spear and atlatl; and the people began to construct pithouses. These innovations added stability to Anasazi life, although gathering wild plants remained an important part of everyday life. The use of

Preceding pages: Freshly fallen snow covers the landscape at White House Ruin, Canyon de Chelly National Monument. Giant patina draperies stain the overhang of the cave sheltering the ruin.
PHOTO BY TOM TILL

Left: Keet Seel, with 155 rooms and six kivas, was discovered in 1895 by Al and Richard Wetherill and is one of the largest and best preserved cliff dwellings in North America. Keet Seel is located at Navajo National Monument.
PHOTO BY LARRY ULRICH

Right: Betatakin, Navajo National Monument, is a Kayenta Anasazi ruin protected in an alcove measuring 452 feet high, 370 feet wide and 135 feet deep. Betatakin is a Navajo word meaning "ledge house." The Navajo are not descendants of the Anasazi and entered the region long after the Anasazi abandoned the area.
PHOTO BY JEFF GNASS

The Anasazi Continued...

pottery allowed for better storage of surplus food for future use, and so the Anasazi became less vulnerable to climactic cycles.

The Pueblo I stage began around A.D. 700 and lasted until A.D. 900. Toward the end of this period, pithouses were beginning to be replaced by above ground dwellings. Although plainware was still predominant, painted pottery emerged with black-on-white, red-on-orange and black-on-red motifs appeared. There is some evidence that agriculture increased in importance and sophistication.

During Pueblo II, from A.D. 900 to 1100, pottery designs became bolder and kivas, communal rooms used for special purposes, began appearing in most villages. It was during this stage that populations began to increase and small villages appeared over a wide range.

The Pueblo III stage, from A.D. 1100 to 1300, found the Anasazi building larger and larger masonry villages, some which were several stories tall, frequently in the shelter of caves or on mesa tops that were easy to defend.

This suggests a new threat from outside forces, perhaps nomadic groups that were ancestors to the Utes and Paiutes. Pottery, jewelry and basket making were refined and trade with neighboring cultures intensified. However, it is at the end of the Pueblo III stage, for reasons that are still not completely understood, western Anasazi sites, including the entire San Juan area, were largely abandoned while the eastern Anasazi sites experienced rapid expansion that lasted into the Pueblo IV stage.

The Pueblo IV stage, from A.D. 1300 until the arrival of the Spanish in 1598, found the Anasazi in northern regions moving south to join the Hopis and Zunis. The existing eastern Anasazi pueblos continued to grow into larger settlements that often housed hundreds, and sometimes thousands, of people.

Of the many distinct Anasazi sites, Chaco in northwest New Mexico was the earliest to leave the Basketmaker III stage and to enter the Pueblo stages. Chaco Canyon was the center of Anasazi civilization by A.D. 900,

and several great houses, roads, and irrigation systems had already been built. At its height, Chaco Canyon may have housed thousands of people, although most evidence points to a majority of occupation occurring on a seasonal basis, with a smaller year round population. Three major building styles were developed: outlying villages of simpler styles thought to be homes for related family groups; Great Towns with huge room blocks that were carefully planned and built in coordinated stages with multiple levels up to 5 stories high; and Great Houses that also possessed large plazas, some with great kivas that also were carefully planned and constructed.

Above: Grand Kiva, Casa Rinconada at Chaco Canyon, Chaco Culture National Historical Park, New Mexico.
PHOTO BY LARRY ULRICH

Chaco Anasazi were accomplished jewelry and ornament makers, producing exquisite turquoise items that are among the finest examples of Pueblo arts and crafts. Chacoans actively engaged in trade with other Anasazi groups and other Southwestern Indian cultures. The Chaco population reached its height in the early A.D. 1100's and peaked around A.D. 1130. Twenty years later, following a long period of very little precipitation, the Chaco people abandoned the region, and moved to more hospitable areas.

The ruins at Chaco Canyon were first discovered by Americans in 1849, when Lt. James Simpson of the United States Army led a military action against Navajo's raiding in the area. Richard Wetherill, as leader of the Hyde Exploring Expedition from 1896 to 1900, was responsible for the earliest excavations at Chaco Canyon. In 1907, Chaco was designated as a national monument. In 1980, after the discovery of large outlying areas of significance, the national monument was expanded

Left: Pueblo Arroyo, Chaco Culture National Historical Park, was constructed using an unusual tri-walled structure. The park's 18 square miles contain eighteen major ruins and countless smaller sites that may have housed up to 5,000 people.
PHOTO BY GEORGE H. H. HUEY

and redesignated as the Chaco Culture National Historical Park.

At Mesa Verde National Park, in southwestern Colorado, Anasazi Basketmaker III (Modified Basket Maker) pithouse remains dating between A.D. 575 and 800 have been discovered, along with mesa top pueblo villages that began to be constructed around A.D. 800. Elaborate cliff dwellings were built during the thirteenth century in the shelter of caves. In all, the park contains more than 4,000 prehistoric sites.

Mesa Top Ruins on Ruins Road Drive offers the chance to study early pithouse dwellings and pueblo villages with subterranean kivas. Sun Point Pueblo, dating around A.D. 1200, is the last of the mesa top developments and shows the first example of a kiva occupying the central plaza of a village. In the early 1200's, residents of Sun Point Pueblo moved off the mesa top to cliff dwellings below, dismantling the village and using its stones and wooden timbers for the construction of new structures. The tremendous amount of labor involved in carrying stone and timber along narrow paths into recesses in the cliff walls leads many to believe that a new threat to the Anasazi's security resulted in the development of defensible cliff dwellings during the final stage of Mesa Verde's development and occupation.

Beneath the mesa top rim are some of the best preserved cliff dwellings in North America. Cliff Palace, the largest cliff dwelling in North America, contains 217 rooms and 23 kivas and is thought to have had a population of around 200-250 people. Long House, with around 150 rooms and 21 kivas, is the second largest ruin within Mesa Verde National Park. Of the park's nearly 600 cliff dwellings, 75 percent contain between one and five rooms. Spruce Tree House, which is visible from a terrace patio outside the park's museum, contained about 114 rooms and eight kivas. Balcony House, a medium sized cliff dwelling 600 feet above the canyon floor has been tree-ring dated, with its first timbers cut in A.D. 1190 and the last cut in A.D. 1282, making this one of the last sites abandoned, as most cliff dwellings in Mesa Verde do not date beyond the late A.D. 1270's.

Although reasons for Anasazi abandonment of Mesa Verde are uncertain, it is thought that a depletion of the natural resources in the area, climactic changes in the region along with prolonged drought, or internal strife may have caused the Mesa Verde Anasazi to leave their homes. Many scientists today believe they moved south to join the Hopi in Arizona, and Zuni, Acoma, Santo Domingo, San Felipe and other Rio Grande Pueblos to the east in what is now the state of New Mexico.

THE ANASAZI CONTINUED...

On December 18, 1888, Richard Wetherill, a Colorado rancher who was riding across the mesa top with his brother-in-law, Charlie Mason, became the first white man to stumble upon the remains of Mesa Verde. Wetherill and other parties explored Mesa Verde sites over the following eighteen years. In 1906, the area achieved national park status. In 1909, Jesse Fewkes of the Smithsonian Institution excavated and stabilized Cliff Palace. In 1978, the park was designated a World Heritage Site, recognizing Mesa Verde National Park's unique anthropological importance.

Ute Mountain Tribal Park, encompassing approximately 125,000 acres on the western and southern boundaries of Mesa Verde, has been set aside by the Ute Mountain Ute Tribe to preserve Anasazi and Ute sites, including Tree House and other cliff dwellings in Lion Canyon that were built around A.D. 1140. Ute Mountain

Left: Square Tower House in winter. Mesa Verde National Park, Colorado.
PHOTO BY JEFF FOOTT

Below: Spruce Tree House in Spruce Tree Canyon, Mesa Verde National Park. Spruce Tree House contains 114 rooms and 8 kivas.
PHOTO BY TOM DANIELSEN

tours are conducted by members of the tribe and reservations in advance are required.

Aztec Ruins, located to the southeast of Mesa Verde National Park in the Animas River Valley, in the San Juan Basin of northern New Mexico, was built in the early 1100's and is believed to have been a community that was part of the greater Chaco culture to the south, and possibly a gathering place for ceremonial functions, as well as a trading center. Aztec Ruins, misnamed by early pioneers who felt they were too sophisticated to have been built by Southwestern Indians and were probably work of the Aztecs of Mexico, show signs of both Chaco and Mesa

Above: Interior view of Cliff Palace at Mesa Verde National Park. Cliff Palace, with 217 rooms and 23 kivas, is the largest cliff dwelling in North America. PHOTO BY TOM DANIELSEN

Verde influences. The main ruin is 360 feet by 275 feet and may have contained around 500 rooms. A great kiva, reconstructed in 1934 by

THE ANASAZI CONTINUED...

Earl Morris, is the largest example of its kind and offers visitors to Aztec Ruins National Monument a chance to experience a kiva much as it must have appeared centuries ago.

Hovenweep National Monument, containing six separate groups of Anasazi ruins, is located in San Juan County, Utah, and Montezuma County, Colorado. The Square Tower and Cajon groups are in Utah, and the Holly Canyon, Hackberry Canyon, Cutthroat Castle and Goodman Point groups are in Colorado. The structures at Hovenweep, a Ute Indian word meaning "deserted valley," were built at canyon heads and next to springs, possibly because the cliffs in the area lacked caves or natural alcoves. Without natural recesses, canyon walls in the region would not have been suitable for building cliff dwellings.

Below: Hovenweep Castle, Hovenweep National Monument. Hovenweep Castle has two towers, two kivas and numerous dwelling rooms.
PHOTO BY TOM TILL

Above: Earl Morris' 1934 reconstruction of The Great Kiva at Aztec Ruins National Monument, New Mexico, is the largest example of its kind.
PHOTO BY TOM TILL

At Hovenweep National Monument the Anasazi farmed the Cajon Mesa from around A.D. 900 to A.D. 1300 and built multi-storied

structures. Some of these are oval, square or circular, while others are "D" shaped. It is believed that population increases and a prolonged period of drought caused Anasazi residents of Hovenweep to completely abandon the region around A.D. 1300. It is believed they moved south to join with other Anasazi who were migrating to Arizona and New Mexico.

Navajo National Monument, on the Navajo Indian Reservation in northeastern Arizona, was home to the Kayenta Anasazi from about A.D. 1250 until around 1300. Even though the area was inhabited for only a short period, the Anasazi cliff dwellings in the Tsegi Canyon

Right: Square Tower Ruin at Hovenweep National Monument is part of the Square Tower Ruin Group, one of six groups of ruins at Hovenweep.
PHOTO BY GEORGE H. H. HUEY

THE ANASAZI CONTINUED...

area of Navajo National Monument are some of the largest ever found. Betatakin, a Navajo word for "ledge house," with more than 135 rooms, and Keet Seel, a Navajo word meaning "broken pottery," with more than 150 rooms and six kivas, were built into huge alcoves in remote Tsegi Canyon's cliffs, far from the Anasazi's fields. Inscription House, in Nitsin Canyon some 35 miles from the visitors' center, is a three-storied structure that contained around eighty rooms and one kiva. By A.D. 1300 the Kayenta Anasazi had left these canyon areas and are thought to have moved to the Hopi Mesas. Rock art found at Betatakin depicts the Hopi Fire Clan symbol, which tends to support Hopi claims to the area as an ancestral site.

In 1895, Richard Wetherill, the Colorado rancher who discovered Mesa Verde in 1888, accompanied by his brother Al and brother-in-law Charlie Mason, was guided to the area containing the ruins of Keet Seel by a Navajo Indian guide. In March of 1909, President Howard Taft established Navajo National Monument to protect the Anasazi ruins of Keet Seel. Within months of the establishment of the national monument, ruins at Betatakin and Inscription House were discovered.

Navajo National Monument is comprised only of the lands that surround its three major ruins. Betatakin and Keet Seel are open to the public. Visits to Inscription House are controlled because of its location and the extremely fragile condition of the ruin.

Also on the Navajo Reservation is Canyon de Chelly National Monument. Its sheer walls and eroded formations have been the home to the Anasazi, Hopi and the Navajo for around 2,000 years. The Anasazi inhabited the region until about A.D. 1300, when they abandoned the area. The Hopi, thought to be descendants of the Anasazi, occupied Canyon de Chelly sporadically until A.D. 1700, when they were replaced by the Navajo who still inhabit the region.

More than 700 prehistoric sites are contained within Canyon de Chelly National Monument, which also includes Canyon del Muerto, or "canyon of the dead," named for the prehistoric Indian burial remains that were discovered there in 1882 by James Stevenson, who was leading an expedition in the area. The prehistoric sites include pithouse remains, pueblos, and cliff dwellings. The cliff dwellings were constructed between A.D. 1100 and A.D. 1300 and include White House Ruins, Antelope House, Mummy Cave Ruin, and numerous other sites. The years of Anasazi occupation

Above: A view from Keet Seel, at Navajo National Monument, showing a unique "street" between rooms of the ruin. President Howard Taft established Navajo National Monument in March of 1909 to protect the Anasazi ruins of Keet Seel.
PHOTO BY GEORGE H. H. HUEY

reflect a more peaceful time in Canyon de Chelly's history, when compared with the history of the region since the white man's arrival in the early 1800's.

The Navajo, fiercely independent and highly aggressive people related to the Apache, began to occupy Canyon de Chelly around 1700. Their uneasy relationships with Europeans and many Indian neighbors, who were the victims of their raids for around 150 years, often drove the Navajo to take refuge from pursuers in Canyon de Chelly. In 1805, the Spanish, under the leadership of Lt. Colonel Antonio Narbona, engaged the Navajo in a day-long battle in Canyon del Muerto. The Navajos took shelter in a cave, since called

Massacre Cave, near the top of the canyon as Spanish forces fired on them from the canyon rim above. When the slaughter ended, more than 100 Indians were dead, including a large number of women and children. Narbona, in his report to the governor of Santa Fe, stated that 115 Navajo were killed, including 90 warriors, and 33 were taken prisoner. There was no mention of women or children. The loss of life to Spanish troops was limited to a single soldier who fell from the cliff to the canyon below.

When the area passed from Spanish and then Mexican control, to the Americans in 1848, the Navajo once again found themselves at odds with the white man. Increased raiding by the Navajo caused white settlers to seek protection. In 1864, Colonel Christopher "Kit" Carson, a famous mountain man and Indian scout, engaged the Navajo at Canyon de Chelly and brought the raiding to an end by marching more than 8,000 Navajo to Fort Sumner, New Mexico, where they remained on the Bosque

Redondo Reservation until allowed to return to their homeland four years later.

Canyon de Chelly National Monument was established on April 1, 1931, and contains more than 130 square miles of land entirely owned by the Navajos, who jointly operate the park with the National Park Service.

Petrified Forest National Park, although best known for its large concentration of petrified logs (formed by fossilization, which turns wood into stone), has hundreds of prehistoric Indian sites that range from the Desert Archaic culture

to the Anasazi and date from around 1050 B.C. to A.D. 1400. Campsite remains of the Desert Archaic culture, pithouse dwellings of the Basketmaker Anasazi, and multi-room pueblos of the Pueblo Anasazi are all found within the park's confines. Puerco Pueblo, near the Puerco River, was inhabited by the Anasazi until about A.D. 1400 and contained more than 100 rooms. Agate House, a partially restored pueblo also found in the park, was constructed with the petrified wood the park is famous for. The Anasazi of the Petrified Forest did not leave the area until around A.D. 1400, a late date for the western Anasazi, at which time they are thought to have moved to the Hopi Mesas or to other pueblos to the east.

The petrified logs were a mystery to the Southwestern Indians who lived in the vicinity of the Petrified Forest. Major John Wesley Powell, on one of his expeditions through the Colorado Plateau, noted that the Paiutes believed the petrified logs were arrow shafts of the thunder god, Shinuav, while the Navajo in the area were convinced the logs were the bones of the monster Yiesto, the "Great Giant" who had been killed by their ancestors upon their arrival in the region. The Indians made use of the petrified wood by carving tools from the stone. It is unknown whether they ever realized that the elements they carved had once been wood.

Below: White House Ruin in fall, Canyon de Chelly National Monument. Canyon de Chelly has been home to Anasazi, Hopi and Navajo farmers over the past 2,000 years.
PHOTO BY DICK DIETRICH

THE ANASAZI CONTINUED...

Basketmaker Anasazi at Bandelier National Monument, on the Pajarito Plateau in northern New Mexico, are thought to have entered the region during the first century A.D. They lived in pithouses, hunted game, gathered native plants, and grew crops of corn, squash, melons and beans. Evidence exists of even earlier Paleo-Indian hunters and Archaic hunters and gatherers who had a presence in the region for thousands of years before the arrival of the Anasazi. These people traveled the Pajarito Plateau in search of plants and animals to support their nomadic existences. The Anasazi were the first group to establish permanent communities at Bandelier, sometime around A.D. 500.

As the Anasazi communities at Chaco and Mesa Verde were reaching their zenith, the people at Bandelier were still part of a much

Left: Agate House, Petrified Forest National Park, is an Anasazi structure built with petrified logs. The park has hundreds of prehistoric sites from the Desert Archaic culture to the Anasazi that date from around 1050 B.C. to A.D. 1400.
PHOTO BY TOM DANIELSEN

simpler time. Mud and grass shelters and single room block and mud homes were built in enclaves that seldom had more than twenty rooms. Hundreds of these enclaves have been discovered on the plateau, some which appear to have been occupied for only a short period of time, which leads scholars to believe the population moved often in order to be near new crops.

As the Anasazi began to leave their Chaco and Mesa Verde homelands, around A.D. 1300, new dwellings began to be constructed at Bandelier that were greatly influenced by Chacoan and Mesa Verde architecture. The soft volcanic tuff of the canyon walls was utilized to build larger pueblos on the canyon bottom. Tyuonyi, a

Above: Ceremonial Cave at Bandelier National Monument. Caves in the base of Bandelier cliffs were created by rapidly cooling lava flows.
PHOTO BY GEORGE H. H. HUEY

multi-storied pueblo from this period that contained around 400 rooms and a large central plaza, was built in the open, away from the sheltering cliffs in Frijoles Canyon.

Long House, named for its 800 foot length, was multi-storied and built with viga holes that anchored roof beams to the cliff surface. Two or three rows of rooms extended outward from the cliff face. In all, several thousand sites have been identified within Bandelier National Monument's boundaries.

The area was abandoned by the Anasazi in the early 1500's, although there were no major climactic disasters to cause the exodus. It is thought Bandelier's inhabitants moved to other pueblos in the Rio Grande Valley, probably the Cochiti and San Ildefonso pueblos.

Bandelier was named for Adolph Bandelier, a Swiss-born adventurer, who discovered the Frijoles Canyon ruins with a Cochiti guide named Juan Jose Montoya in October of 1880. Adolph Bandelier, who had no formal training in archeology, traveled throughout North and South America recording prehistoric ruins.

In February of 1916, a presidential proclamation by President Wilson established Bandelier National Monument to protect and preserve the ruins and relics of Bandelier. In the 1930's, the Civilian Conservation Corps built a road into the canyon and constructed the park's Visitor Center, guest lodge and several other buildings.

Left: Tyuonyi ruin, Bandelier National Monument. Construction at Tyuonyi, a large multi-storied pueblo, began in the thirteenth century. It was built in the open, away from the sheltering cliffs, in Frijoles Canyon. When completed it contained around 400 rooms and a large central plaza.
PHOTO BY GEORGE H. H. HUEY

THE ANASAZI CONTINUED...

Pithouse remains in Pecos National Historical Park in north-central New Mexico establish Anasazi inhabitants in this area at least as early as A.D. 800. It is thought Anasazi from the northwest joined those living at Pecos in the early twelfth century and began to build multi-storied pueblos. Pecos Pueblo became an important Anasazi trading center.

When the Spanish conquistadors first arrived at Pecos in 1540, Pecos was a four to five story fortress that sheltered around 2,000 people. It was a major center of trade between the Pueblo Indians and the Plains Indians. Spanish missions were established at Pecos starting in 1598 to convert the Pueblo Indians to Christianity. The largest mission church was finished by Franciscan Father Andrés Juarez in 1625, the remains of which lay beneath the ruins of a church built in 1717. During the Pueblo Revolt in 1680, the mission was destroyed by the Pueblo Indians and the Spanish were driven south to El Paso, Texas. The Pecos people then reclaimed the area and built a kiva in the ruins of the living quarters of the church.

In 1692, the Spaniards regained control of New Mexico, and Pecos entered into a new era

Below: Pecos Pueblo, Pecos National Historical Park. When the Spaniards arrived in 1540 Pecos Pueblo was four to five stories tall and contained more than 650 rooms and 22 kivas.
PHOTO BY GEORGE H. H. HUEY

Right: Long House, Bandelier National Monument. Long House ruin is 800 feet long and was multi-storied with two or three rooms that extended outward from the cliff face.
PHOTO BY GEORGE H. H. HUEY

of problems. Comanche raids and European diseases decimated the population until there were only around 200 Pueblo Indians remaining at Pecos in 1786. By 1838, the population had dwindled down to a mere seventeen people, who then moved to Jemez Pueblo, forever abandoning the once powerful Pecos Pueblo. In 1965, Pecos Pueblo was established as a national monument and in 1990 the area was designated Pecos National Historical Park.

The Anasazi are known to have inhabited sites in the Grand Canyon, although the area was primarily a Hakatayan culture region. There is evidence of some Basketmaker II utilization of the canyon although the majority of Anasazi sites date between A.D. 1050 and 1150. Most Grand Canyon sites are one or two rooms, or are

granaries, although there are larger villages both at the bottom of the Canyon and on the

Above: Sunrise at Hilltop Ruin, Grand Canyon National Park. The Anasazi built villages at the bottom of the Canyon and on the rim. PHOTO BY TOM TILL

rim. The Tusayan Ruin, west of Desert View on the South Rim, is a two-story "U" shaped

Anasazi pueblo of around 30 rooms and dates from A.D. 1170 to 1205. Walhalla Glades Ruin on the Canyon's North Rim was occupied sometime after A.D. 1050, and Bright Angel Pueblo, with six rooms and a kiva at the bottom of the canyon near the Colorado River, was built in two phases between about A.D. 1050 and A.D. 1140.

The Anasazi occupied Zion National Park from about A.D. 500 until 1200. Although they built none of the large pueblos or cliff dwellings found in other areas of the Four Corner states, a small dwelling and several granaries have been uncovered. The northern areas of what today is Zion National Park may have been occupied during this period by people of the Fremont culture, who lived in pithouses and surface dwellings similar to early Anasazi pueblos. There is little evidence of interaction between these two groups.

The Anasazi abandoned the Zion National Park area earlier than most of their northern territory for reasons that are still unknown, but may include problems with other Indian tribes in the area.

Canyonlands National Park in southeastern Utah features Anasazi pueblos that were not as elaborately constructed as those found in the Four Corners region but were multi-room

Above: An Anasazi granary in Zion National Park. Although the Anasazi occupied Zion National Park from about A.D. 500 until 1200, they built none of the large pueblos or cliff dwellings found in other areas of the Four Corners.
PHOTO BY TOM TILL

structures and were sometimes sheltered in caves, such as Tower Ruin in The Needles. The Anasazi in Canyonlands reached the peak of their culture between A.D. 1000 and 1200. Here, as in Zion and other northern areas of Anasazi territory, Anasazi co-existed

Left: Anasazi dwelling ruin at Natural Bridges National Monument in southeastern Utah. The Anasazi inhabited White and Armstrong canyons of Cedar Mesa from about A.D. 100 to 1300.
PHOTO BY GEORGE H. H. HUEY

with the Fremont culture, a less sophisticated group that was found throughout the northern two-thirds of Utah and Colorado during the Classic Pueblo times.

Natural Bridges National Monument, located in southeastern Utah, contains three spectacular natural bridges, Rainbow Bridge, Sipapu and Kachina, which were carved by streams millions of years ago. Rainbow Bridge is the largest natural bridge in the world. The Anasazi were attracted to the area, probably because of an abundance of water and for the shelter provided by the canyons. They inhabited small pueblos in the White and Armstrong canyons of Cedar Mesa from about A.D. 100 to 1300.

Below: Anasazi ruin in the Grand Gulch Primitive Area, Utah. The Four Corners region has countless Anasazi sites, not all of which are found within national parks or monuments.
PHOTO BY JEFF FOOTT

Horsecollar Ruin, nestled in one of the cliffs of White Canyon, is the largest Anasazi site in Natural Bridges National Monument.

The Four Corners area, which includes parts of Arizona, Colorado, New Mexico and Utah, has countless Anasazi sites, not all of which are found within national parks or monuments. When visiting remote locations, use caution, check with local authorities for rules and regulations, and do not disturb any site or remove any artifacts.

Right: Pictographs, Canyonlands National Park. The Anasazi and Fremont cultures both inhabited the Canyonlands area. The Anasazi reached their peak at Canyonlands between A.D. 1000 to 1200.
PHOTO BY CHUCK PLACE

THE SINAGUA

The Sinagua occupied areas near Flagstaff and the San Francisco Peaks down to the Verde Valley from about A.D. 500 until the early fourteenth century. They lived a peaceful existence in timber pithouses, growing crops, hunting game and gathering wild foods. They were involved in trade between the Hohokam, Anasazi (Hisatsinom), Mogollon and other Southwestern cultures. Copper bells and parrots from Mexico, turquoise from New Mexico, shells from the Pacific coast and Gulf of California, Hohokam and Kayenta Anasazi pottery, and pipestone (red argillite) from the Prescott area have all been found in Sinagua sites. Sinagua trade products were probably salt mined near Camp Verde, ornaments fashioned from turquoise and pipestone, or from shells, and woven cotton textiles.

The Sinagua were named by scientist Dr. Harold S. Colton in the 1930's for the Spanish phrase *sin* "without" and *agua* "water." Dr. Colton believed the Sinagua, farmers who inhabited the area around the San Francisco Peaks beginning about A.D. 500, to be a distinct culture that was unrelated to the Hohokam, Anasazi and Mogollon. Other scholars feel they were possibly a branch of the Mogollon, a part of the Western Anasazi, or a minor culture combining traces of the Hohokam, Anasazi and Mogollon cultures. Located in a region that was overlapped by the Hohokam, Mogollon and Anasazi, the Sinagua were at least influenced heavily by elements of these three cultures.

It is important to note that although there still exists controversy among archeologists regarding the origins of the Sinagua, and to a much lesser extent their final disposition at the height of their culture, the Hopi Indians have no doubt that the Sinagua and Anasazi of the region are their ancestral peoples. The term Anasazi is from the Navajo language and means "ancient people who are not us" or "ancient enemies." Anasazi is offensive to the Hopi who call their ancestors the Hisatsinom, which literally means "people of long ago." Currently, many people are endeavoring to change the Anasazi name to the more accurate Hisatsinom in deference to the Hopi.

The Sinagua were involved in trade between Hohokam, Anasazi (Hisatsinom), Mogollon and other Southwestern cultures. Copper bells and parrots from Mexico, turquoise from New Mexico, shells from the Pacific coast and Gulf of California, Hohokam and Kayenta Anasazi pottery, and pipestone (red argillite) from the Prescott area have all been found at Sinagua sites. Sinagua trade products were probably salt mined near Camp Verde, ornaments fashioned from turquoise and pipestone or from shells, and woven cotton textiles. Sinagua pottery and baskets were generally considered rather plain, although the fragile nature of basketry leaves few well-preserved examples; they were probably not a major trade item.

In addition to the exchange of goods between the Sinagua and neighboring cultures, there also appears to be a great deal of social and technological interchange. Hohokam style ball courts have been found at several Sinagua sites including Wupatki and Winona Village; ceremonial kivas normally associated with the Anasazi are in evidence; Hohokam, Anasazi, and Mogollon architectural influence is found throughout Sinagua sites; and Anasazi pottery may have inspired several of the predominant styles of Sinagua painted pottery.

In addition to their role as merchants, the Sinagua were also resourceful farmers, growing crops of corn, beans, squash and cotton. They depended mainly on rainfall to water their crops, since they had few reliable water sources suitable for irrigation. Wild plants were also gathered including hackberry, mesquite beans, prickly-pear fruit, yucca, agave, walnuts and other food stuffs. Of the approximately 240 varieties of plants native to the region, possibly as many as half were used for fuel, medicines, basketry materials, matting, thatching and other purposes; they

Left: Sinagua Rim, Montezuma Well, Montezuma Castle National Monument. Natural spring water filled the bottom of this limestone sinkhole and was used by the Sinagua and the Hohokam to irrigate their crops.
PHOTO BY JEFF GNASS

Right: Tuzigoot, a Sinagua pueblo, caps a limestone-sandstone ridge that overlooks the lush Verde River Valley. The Sinagua abandoned Tuzigoot in the 1400's. Tuzigoot National Monument, Arizona.
PHOTO BY TOM DANIELSEN

were more valuable to the Sinaguan culture than domesticated crops. The Sinagua also used the bow and arrow to hunt small and large game animals including deer, rabbit, pronghorn antelope, beaver and elk. (Elk was found only in the more mountainous regions of the northern Sinagua.)

The Sinagua culture has been divided into two branches, the northern and the southern. The northern Sinagua occupied the area near Flagstaff and the San Francisco Peaks from about A.D. 500 until the early fourteenth century. They lived a peaceful existence in timber pithouses, growing crops, hunting game and gathering wild foods until disaster struck in 1064. A volcano, the remains of which is Sunset Crater, began a series of eruptions that destroyed all vegetation within a two-mile radius of the cone, covering more than 800 square miles of the surrounding area with volcanic ash and cinders. The resulting crater was four hundred feet deep.

With the eruption of the volcano, the Sinagua fled their homes. When they drifted back into the area several years later the soil had been made more suitable for farming by the volcanic ash, which served as a moisture-retaining mulch. The renewed soil moisture allowed the Sinagua to re-utilize the area and attracted other Indian groups including Hohokam, Anasazi, and Mogollon. These more advanced cultures influenced the Sinagua, who absorbed their customs and skills. Masonry pueblos of

the Anasazi style began to replace Sinagua pithouses, although construction of pithouses continued. The Sinagua and the new arrivals appear to have blended peacefully.

Above: Apache plume, aspens and Sunset Crater at Sunset Crater National Monument. In 1064, Sunset Crater began a series of eruptions that covered around 800 square miles of the surrounding region with cinders and ash, causing the northern Sinagua to flee their homes. PHOTO BY LARRY ULRICH

With the new skills the Sinagua acquired, they built the 60-70 room Elden Pueblo near present-day Flagstaff, where they lived from around A.D. 1070 until sometime around A.D. 1275. Turkey Hill Pueblo northeast of Flagstaff, a masonry pueblo of more than 30 rooms, was occupied during this same time period.

Among the best preserved, and the most extensive, northern Sinagua ruins are the multi-storied pueblos found thirty miles north of Flagstaff at Wupatki National Monument. Wupatki's 56 square mile area contains more than 2600 prehistoric sites, a majority of which are post-eruption, although pithouses have been excavated, covered by volcanic ash, that pre-date the eruption. Many of the later sites show the influences of the Anasazi, Hohokam and Mogollon who moved into the area after Sunset Crater's eruption.

Wupatki National Monument contains excavated ruins of thirteen structures. Nalakihu, Hopi for "long house," has ten ground floor and several second story rooms at the base of the trail leading uphill to the Citadel Ruin, which had around thirty rooms. Remains of pottery found at these neighboring sites suggests their inhabitants were of different cultures prior to their relocation next to one another.

Wukoki, two miles east of the Wupatki ruin, is a three story structure with seven or eight

rooms. Lomaki, another pueblo located within the national monument, has been tree ring dated with the earliest timber cut in A.D. 1192, and the latest cutting dated at 1205. Absence of later cutting dates probably means this site was abandoned by A.D. 1225.

Wupatki National Monument's largest site is its namesake, Wupatki Pueblo. Wupatki, a Hopi word meaning "tall house," has more than 100 excavated rooms and several unique features including a Hohokam style ball court, the only example in the Southwest constructed of stone masonry, and a large amphitheater.

Excavation work at Wupatki has led to other important archeological discoveries. The skeletal remains of 42 macaws were unearthed, which leads scientists to believe that these colorful birds, not just their feathers, were trade items from Mexico. Bowls of cotton and cotton seed were discovered in quantity, along with weaving tools, which supports the theory that cotton was grown in the region and that woven cotton textiles were an important trade item.

Walnut Canyon National Monument, seven miles east of Flagstaff, was occupied by the northern Sinagua from about A.D. 1100 until around 1250. Cliff dwellings include the remains of more than 300 rooms. There are also surface dwellings, constructed by the Sinagua on the mesa above the cliff dwellings, and pithouse remains from an earlier culture. The Walnut Canyon ruins were not widely known until the Atlantic & Pacific Railway reached northern Arizona in the 1880's. These ruins proved a popular tourist spot and looters, known as pot hunters, removed many artifacts that would have helped archeologists better understand the Sinagua culture. In 1915, the pillaging was ended with the creation of Walnut Canyon National Monument.

The southern Sinagua appeared in the Verde Valley area around A.D. 700. The area's lower elevations offered a mild climate, long growing season and a steady water supply from the Verde River, which flowed all year. Leading a peaceful existence, early southern Sinagua grew crops, gathered wild foods and hunted game while living in traditional pithouses. In the ninth century small pueblos appeared. During this period the Hohokam were also found in the area. Remnants of irrigation canals for watering their crops still remain.

Tree ring dating of beams found in the ruins at Palatki and Honanki, near Sedona, place the

Left: Lomaki Ruin, Wupatki National Monument, at sunrise. Wupatki National Monument contains the excavated ruins of thirteen structures.
PHOTO BY TOM DANIELSEN

Right: Montezuma Castle, a late stage dwelling of the Sinagua constructed in the thirteenth century, was erroneously named after the famous Aztec chief. Montezuma Castle National Monument.
PHOTO BY GEORGE H. H. HUEY

Above: Sinagua ruin, Walnut Canyon National Monument was created in 1915 to end looting of Walnut Canyon by pot hunters in the late 1800's and early 1900's.
PHOTO BY DICK DIETRICH

development of these cliff dwellings between A.D. 1130 and 1300. The northern Sinagua began to arrive in the Verde Valley area during the early fourteenth century after a long period of drought, when winds had eroded the top soil of farm lands in the north.

Tuzigoot National Monument, a stone pueblo of more than 100 rooms overlooking the Verde River near Clarkdale, has provided valuable insight into Sinagua history. More than 400 gravesites have been found, with nearly half of the bodies belonging to infants and children, many of which were simply scooped out of nearby trash mounds. High infant mortality may have been one reason why the Sinagua

left the area in the 1400's.

Montezuma Castle National Monument is comprised of two distinct locations: Montezuma Castle, two five-story pueblos built into the cliffs above Beaver Creek in the Verde Valley; and Montezuma Well, a limestone sink partly filled with water from an underground spring.

The Montezuma Well area features an excavated pithouse, rooms inside the sink, and two pueblos located near the rim. Montezuma Castle's two ruins have walls of limestone blocks. The upper ruin has twenty rooms high in an alcove in the cliff's wall, and can only be reached by two narrow trails that would have been easy to defend. The lower ruin, at the base of the cliff, has forty-five rooms that could only be reached by climbing ladders.

Although the Sinagua appeared to be secure in their Verde Valley settlements, for unknown reasons they completely abandoned the area around A.D. 1425. Scientists speculate this disappearance may have been the result of drought, warfare, or possibly disease. It is also believed they moved to the northwest where they may have joined certain Hopi clans.

Following pages: Palatki Ruin, in Red Canyon near Sedona, Arizona consists of stone structures that were occupied by the southern Sinagua from about A.D. 1150 until around 1250.
PHOTO BY TOM DANIELSEN

THE SALADO

Inhabiting the Tonto Basin in central Arizona for a relatively short period between A.D. 1150 and around A.D. 1450, the Salado culture was named for the Salt River (Rio Salado in Spanish) that was central to their way of life. Considered a minor culture by most archeologists, their origins are still debated by many. The first to identify the Salado as a separate culture was anthropologist Erich Schmidt, who studied Armer Ruin, a fourteenth century village exposed as Roosevelt Lake receded during a drought in 1925, as well as Togetzoge, a pueblo near Miami, Arizona, with around 120 rooms. The excavations at Togetzoge revealed new red-on-buff pottery Schmidt called Gila Polychrome, which he felt introduced a new culture.

In 1930, archeologist Harold Gladwin was the first to name this new culture. Gladwin felt the Salado sites represented a distinct and separate culture, although other archeologists including Emil W. Haury, Gladwin's associate at the Gila Pueblo Foundation in Globe, Arizona, believed the Salado were a combination of other cultures, in Haury's opinion the Mogollon and Anasazi. Others feel they were a Hohokam and Sinagua cultural mix; an outpost group from Mexico; or Hohokam who had moved into the region, as evidenced by many similarities between these two cultures.

By the appearance of the Salado culture, Southwestern cultures were so intermixed that it is hard to distinguish where one culture ended and another began, and whether this was a result of trade and exchange of ideas, or assimilation of one group by another.

The Salado, thought to have moved into the Tonto Basin from the upper Little Colorado River area sometime around A.D. 1150, lived in above ground pueblos that show Hohokam influence. Adobe mud was used as mortar in masonry construction, and platform mounds of earth and trash, normally associated with the Hohokam, are present at some Salado sites. Some believe the Hohokam were influenced by the Salado, who may have peacefully joined the Hohokam in the middle fourteenth century after abandoning their Tonto Basin homes.

The Salado hunted deer, pronghorn antelope, bighorn sheep and small game, gathered wild foods, and grew crops including corn, beans and squash. These crops were irrigated using canals, which reveals a strong Hohokam influence.

Besh-Ba-Gowah, located near Globe, Arizona contained around 200 rooms and was occupied from A.D. 1225 to 1400. Gila Pueblo, located just a mile from Besh-Ba-Gowah on the opposite side of Pinal Creek, had around 400 rooms. Togetzoge, a pueblo near Miami, Arizona, had around 120 rooms. Tonto National Monument, near Roosevelt Lake, contains Salado dwellings in two caves. The Upper Ruin has 40 rooms and is around 250 feet above the Lower Ruin, which has 19 rooms and is about 350 feet above the valley.

The Salado abandoned their Southwestern homes in the mid 1400's and, as with other Indian cultures of the period, considerable debate exists as to their final disposition. Some archeologists believe they joined the Zuni, Hopi, or both, while others feel they may have moved into northern Mexico.

The Salado culture was first defined by Erich Schmidt, a German doctoral student from Columbia University. Schmidt was sent by the American Museum of Natural History in New York to work at a ruin near Superior, Arizona, in 1925. As the water level of Roosevelt Lake lowered in response to a drought, Armer Ruin was exposed. News of the ruin attracted national headlines with stories of a 2,000-5,000 year old town, with buildings larger than those on Park Avenue in New York. The site was later dated to the fourteenth century. Erich Schmidt spent much of his time working at Togetzoge, near Superior, Arizona, where he identified pottery he named Gila Polychrome. Schmidt established the groundwork for Harold Gladwin to identify the Salado culture in 1930.

Right: Lower Ruin at Tonto National Monument has 19 rooms and the Lower Ruin Annex has an additional eleven rooms. The Upper Ruin has around 40 rooms.
PHOTO BY JEFF GNASS

Left: Besh-Ba-Gowah Pueblo, Globe, Arizona. This Salado ruin contains around 200 rooms and was excavated and partially restored in the late 1930's by Irene Vickery.
PHOTO BY MICHAEL COLLIER

The decline of the Native American people and their influence in the Southwest began when the first Europeans, Spanish conquistadors, arrived in the Southwest in 1540. The Pueblo Indians had alternately attempted to exist peacefully with the less than gracious intruders, then expelled them in the 1680 Pueblo Revolt. Nomadic bands were slightly more successful, with the Comanches, Apaches, Navajos and Utes continuing to raid both Pueblo Indians and the white settlers until the Americans arrived following the Mexican War. The Anglos had less influence over the Pueblo Indians than the Spaniards, but were entirely successful in eliminating threats from the hostile raiders. By the late 1800's, the Indians of the Southwest were relegated to reservations.

Southwestern Indians are direct ancestors of nomadic tribes that crossed the Bering Straits during the long period of glaciation that ended concurrently with the ending of the Pleistocene Epoch, or Ice Age, more than eleven thousand years ago. They arrived at different times, and are undoubtedly from several different original groups. The major tribes of historic times are related in part to prehistoric Pueblo cultures, Plains Indians, and Athabascan nomadic tribes from Canada.

Southwestern Indian tribes of historic times include Acoma, Apache, Caddo, Chemehuevi, Cochiti, Cocopah, Comanche, Havasupai, Hopi, Hualapai, Isleta, Jemez, Kiowa, Laguna, Mohave, Maricopa, Nambre, Navajo, Paiute, Picuris, Pima, Pojaque, San Felipe, San Ildefonso, San Juan, Sandia, Santa Ana, Santa Clara, Santo Domingo, Taos, Tesque, Tohono O'otham, Ute, Yavapai, Yaqui, Yuma, Zia, and Zuñi.

The Navajo, Athabascans who migrated into the Southwest from Canada several centuries before the arrival of the Spaniards, are the largest of all Native American tribes. They were nomadic hunter-gatherers who are closely related to the Apache. They chose the region of their current reservation as their homeland. Today, the Navajo Indian Reservation covers a vast territory, around 16 million acres of land, that includes portions of Arizona, Utah and New Mexico. The reservation is home to around 160,000 Navajos.

Prior to the arrival of the Spanish, the Navajo conducted frequent raids against the Pueblo Indians and their other neighbors. The Utes made continual efforts to force the Navajo from northern New Mexico but were unsuccessful.

The Navajo often chose the intricate canyons of Canyon de Chelly as a refuge from intruders and pursuers seeking retaliation for their raids. The entire area was fortress-like in its natural state. By 1805, the Spanish had reached the end of their patience with the Navajo who, like the Comanche and Apache, had proven much harder to control than the semi-peaceful Pueblo Indians. A Spanish detachment, under the leadership of Lt. Colonel Antonio Narbona, was sent by the governor of New Mexico to put an end to the Navajo raiding.

After a lengthy pursuit the Spanish engaged the Navajo at Canyon del Muerto in Canyon de Chelly. In a day-long battle, Navajo warriors, women, and children took shelter in a cave, now aptly called Massacre Cave, near the top of the canyon. The Spanish forces fired on the warriors, and defenseless Indian women and children, from a point on the canyon rim above. When the slaughter was over, more than 100 Indians, mostly women and children, were dead. Narbona, in his official report to the governor in Santa Fe, had an entirely different account of the confrontation.

Narbona stated that 115 Navajo were killed, including 90 warriors, and that 33 were taken prisoner. No mention was made of the women and children, probably a wise decision on Narbona's part since the Spanish Crown did not seek the genocide of their Indian subjects. Colonel Narbona later substantiated his claims with a package that contained the ears of 84 Indians, with an apology for the missing pairs. The captives were enslaved by the Spaniards.

Left: Havasu Falls, Havasupai Indian Reservation. Havasu Canyon, in the southwestern corner of the Grand Canyon, was severely damaged by spring floods in 1993. Havasu Canyon has been home to indians for more than 1,000 years. The current residents, the Havasupai, whose name means "the people that live where the waters are blue-green," inherited the canyon from earlier residents.
PHOTO BY JEFF GNASS

Right: View from Massai Point, Rhyolite Canyon, Chiricahua National Monument. The Chiricahua Apache lived in these canyons for centuries, until encroachment by early American settlers drove them from the area in the late 1880's.
PHOTO BY JEFF GNASS

The loss of life to the Spanish troops in the one-sided encounter was limited to a single man who fell from the cliff to the canyon floor.

The Navajo had learned the ineffectiveness of arrows and stones against the rifles of the white man, and kept a relatively low profile throughout the remaining years of Spanish influence. The Navajo, like the Apache, had always lead an existence supplemented by raids on other tribes, and now, on the foreign intruders. When the area passed from Spanish and Mexican control, to the Americans in 1848, the Navajo found themselves once again at odds with the white man.

Increased Navajo raiding against American settlers encroaching on Navajo tribal lands caused the white settlers to call for retaliation. In 1863, U.S. Army Brigadier General James Henry Carleton sent Christopher "Kit" Carson, mountain man and Indian scout, north with orders to engage the Navajo. Carson, a Colonel of the volunteers, was ordered by the ruthless Carleton: "All Indian men of that tribe are to be killed whenever and wherever you find them; the women and children will not be harmed, but you will take them prisoners." Carson's orders were clear; he was not to make any attempt at peace but to kill the Navajo men in their entirety.

In the summer of 1863, Carson gathered 736 volunteers consisting of Spanish and American settlers, Utes, Zuñi, and some Hopi

Indians–all unsympathetic to the Navajo–and set out to systematically complete this task. On route to Canyon de Chelly, Carson and his

Above: Acoma Pueblo, one of the oldest continually inhabited villages in America. In 1540 Spaniards killed around 100 Acoma men in an attempt to scale the more than 400 foot high cliffs to the pueblo. In 1598, the pueblo submitted to Spanish rule, but soon killed the governor of New Mexico's nephew. His death was avenged by the killing of 100 Acoma men and the kidnapping of 60 young girls, who were sold into slavery in Mexico.
PHOTO BY TOM TILL

volunteers burned Navajo houses, killed their sheep, and destroyed their fields. His attacks were so effective that, by September, large

numbers of Navajos began to surrender. Many sought refuge at Fort Defiance, where they were given food and protection. Bands of Navajos fled in all directions. Some joined with other tribes and others took refuge in remote areas to the north. By January of 1864, the only Navajos still at large were hiding in the Canyon de Chelly area.

When Kit Carson arrived at the mouth of Canyon de Chelly in January of 1864, the battle was all but won. The Navajos had long used the canyon area as a summer home, but were ill-equipped to survive winter in the area. Carson, to his credit, sent dispatches to Carleton arguing there were too few Indians left in the canyon to justify hardships his troops faced during a harsh winter campaign. Carleton, unfortunately for the remaining Navajos, felt a decisive victory would achieve a lasting psychological effect on Navajos everywhere, and ordered Carson to proceed into the Canyon.

By April of 1864, cold and hunger forced the final surrender of the Navajos in Canyon de Chelly. More than 8,000 Navajo men, women and children began what became known as the "Long Walk" to their place of exile at Fort Sumner, New Mexico. Bosque Redondo, the new reservation, was a treeless and barren land where thousands of Navajos later died from exposure and the white man's diseases. After four years, the United State's Army acknowledged their error in judgement and let the Navajos return to the location of their present reservation.

The Hopi Indians, abbreviated from Hopituh Shi-nu-mu, which means "the peaceful people," are the only remaining pueblo dwellers in Arizona. The Hopi have occupied their domain for hundreds of years, in villages on top of the high, barren mesas in northern Arizona.

Thomas V. Keam, an Englishman, started a trading post in 1878 near the three Hopi mesas in an area that came to be known as Keams Canyon. Keams named the mesas "First Mesa," "Second Mesa," and "Third Mesa," in the opposite order the Hopi referred to their ancestral sites. In ancient times, these mesas, the three southern prongs of Black Mesa, provided the Hopi with natural protection from their enemies.

Left: Snow covers Spider Rock and Canyon de Chelly, Canyon de Chelly National Monument. In the winter of 1864, Kit Carson forced the final surrender of the Navajo in Canyon de Chelly.
PHOTO BY JEFF GNASS

Right: Totem Pole and Yei-Bi-Chei in Monument Valley, Navajo Tribal Park, Arizona.
PHOTO BY JEFF GNASS

In 1543, Spaniards, under the command of Don Pedro de Tovar, first visited the Hopi. They brought gifts and established a camp near Kawaiokuh, which today is a ruin. From the Hopi, the Spaniards learned of the Colorado River and the Grand Canyon. Don Pedro de Tovar ordered Captain Garcia de Cardenas north to search for the Canyon and the river. The Spanish, unimpressed by the region and its lack of precious minerals, did not visit the Hopi again for another 40 years. When they returned, they attempted to convert the Hopi to Christianity, and continued to try and do so until the Hopi joined other Pueblo Indians in the Pueblo Revolt of 1680. Spanish intervention meant little to the Hopi; they were uninterested in the white man's God, and their remote and arid region did not attract many white settlers.

Old Oraibi vies with the Hopi village of Acoma, in New Mexico, for the distinction of being the oldest continuously occupied village in North America. Both were established about 1100 A.D. Old Oraibi was one of the largest Hopi villages until 1906, when arguments over education of Hopi children brought about the founding of Hotevilla, Bacabi, and New Oraibi on Third Mesa.

Above: Hopi kachina mask of Wukogle at Amerind Institute. PHOTO BY JACK DYKINGA

The Hopi are concerned with preservation of their lands. For many centuries they have been surrounded by the Navajo, who were their traditional enemies. Through a series of treaties, the Navajo and Hopi have attempted unsuccessfully to resolve their territorial conflicts for decades. Ownership disputes over these lands continue in Washington today.

The Hopi social organization is based upon the clan system, with strong ties to the mother. Homes are built adjacent to the mother's home, and men join their wife's clan after marriage. Women own the houses, food, seeds for planting, the springs, wells and their gardens. Men do the hunting, farming, herding, and yarn and leather work. An important aspect of the social structure is curing, which is under the control of medicine societies known as kachina. All Hopi are members of one of the numerous kachina cults.

The Hopi conduct their ceremonies to ensure the proper passage of the seasons, promote fertility in plants and animals, encourage rain, and to ensure hunting success. Many of these elaborate presentations are open to visitors. The Snake dances are among the best known and most involved. Men and boys of the Snake and Antelope fraternities emerge from their kivas, painted and costumed, and search the surrounding countryside for four days gathering snakes. On the day of the Snake

dance, Antelope priests line up in the plaza and await the arrival of Snake priests. Upon the arrival of the Snake priests, gourds are rattled to emulate the sound of rattlesnakes, and the priests begin a deep sonorous chorus. As the chorus reaches a climax, the Snake men form groups of three and reach into a cottonwood bough, where a priest, who is hidden inside, hands them a snake. The snake is placed in the mouth of the Snake man, while his two assistants trail behind to control the snake. As many as 70 or 80 snakes may be involved in the ceremony. As the ceremony continues, Hopi women sprinkle corn meal on the snakes and the dancers. When all of the snakes are freed and placed within a circle, they dart in all directions. Pandemonium ensues among the Hopi and visitors alike, until all of the snakes have been collected. The Snake men then rush out of the village and down the trails to free the snakes. When the ceremony ends, villagers relax and a four day festival begins.

Long before the arrival of the first Europeans, the Apache Indians, nomadic Athabascan bands, occupied the Southwest. Inhabiting an area from the eastern slopes of the Rocky Mountains, west to the base of the Sangre de Cristo Mountains (near Cimmaron and Las Vegas), and from the northern plains of the Colorado Plateau south to Texas and Mexico, Apaches led a simple existence. In centuries prior to the arrival of the Spanish Franciscan priests, the Apaches were peaceful tribes that depended upon small and large game hunting,

some simple farming, and the wild foods they gathered from the land.

Living in permanent villages, the Apaches conducted extensive bison hunts, grew maize

Above: Blanket and pueblo walls at Taos Pueblo, New Mexico. The Taos Indians have lived in Taos Pueblo, the largest existing multi-storied Pueblo structure in the United States, for nearly 1,000 years. PHOTO BY TOM TILL

and harvested great quantities of mescal. When it was necessary, they could literally "live off the land" by harvesting berries, roots, seeds and cactus, and by hunting game animals. The Apaches were extremely healthy and vigorous people before the introduction of the white man's diseases. They were capable of traveling great distances in the summer heat of

the desert, and in the chilling cold of winter in the mountains, with little or no discomfort.

With the Apaches, past and present, women are held in high regard. They are protected, respected and cherished. Girls were given the same training as boys and practiced daily with bows and arrows, slings, and spears. They were taught horseback riding and combat. In times of war, wives were permitted to go on the warpath with husbands.

Contrary to popular belief, the Apache did not scalp their victims. In fact, scalping was introduced to the Southwestern Indians by Spaniards. During the 1830's, Spaniards instituted a scalp-bounty system, an ancient Spanish practice, in which anyone bringing in the scalp of an adult male would be paid $100, an adult female paid $50 and $25 was paid for the scalp of a child.

This practice backfired in many ways. It was impossible to differentiate between an Apache scalp and those of other Indian tribes. Soon even friendly tribes were on the warpath as unscrupulous bounty hunters collected scalps wherever they could. Examining committees found it difficult to differentiate between the hair of Indians and Mexicans, and soon entire Mexican villages were murdered by bounty hunters to collect their grisly rewards. By 1837, the scalp-bounty system had escalated to unbelievable acts of violence and depravity.

James Johnson, a bounty hunter, illustrated the extent these despicable murderers would go to in their quest for profit. Johnson entered the Apache village of Juan Jose, where he was well known, with gifts for the Apache. Inside one sack was a small loaded cannon with its barrel tightly plugged. The Apaches gathered to see the "magic" Johnson had promised. Johnson lit the cannon's fuse with a cigar and calmly walked away, telling the Apache to keep watching the fuse. The cannon exploded, killing or injuring most of the Indians. Johnson and his men then calmly scalped the dead.

When an Apache was killed it obligated their relatives to seek revenge. Most war parties were formed to avenge deaths. The Apache god, Usen, had not commanded the Apache to forgive their enemies. Nor was one life ever considered enough for any Apache killed, often many lives were required to avenge the death of an Apache.

Apache chief Cochise once stated, "Americans began the fight, and now the Americans and Mexicans kill an Apache on sight. I have retaliated with all my might. I have killed ten white men for every Indian slain."

COCHISE, CHIRICAHUA APACHE CHIEF

Cochise was tribal leader of the Chiricahua Apache by the 1860's and was well known by Indians, Mexicans and Americans alike as a fearless warrior. The son-in-law of the famous Apache chief Mangus Coloradas, Cochise was a strong and compassionate leader. Although many were terrified of him, he was considered to be a man of his word to all who knew him.

In 1861, John Ward reported the capture of his stepson by Apaches. Though no evidence linked the abduction to Cochise or his band, a company of Army Infantry, led by Lt. George Bascom, contacted Cochise through an inter-preter and requested Cochise and his followers visit Bascom's camp for a parley.

The Apaches entered a large tent with Bascom and several of his aides. As Cochise explained that he knew nothing of the missing boy, Lt. Bascom's men surrounded the tent. Bascom informed Cochise that he and his group were under arrest. Instantly, Cochise pulled a knife and ripped through the rear wall of the tent, running toward freedom. The soldiers, caught unaware, regained their senses and fired more than 50 shots, but Cochise escaped unharmed.

The six Apaches still in Bascom's tent were unable to escape. The next day Cochise tried to negotiate their release, but Bascom refused to leave the security of his camp. Cochise called

to three men, a stationmaster, a stagecoach driver, and a hostler, who all knew and trusted him. Bascom refused to allow the men to meet with Cochise, but they walked toward him anyway. Cochise moved to grab the men, not intending harm, but to use them to trade for his warriors. As the stationmaster was seized by Indians, the other men panicked and ran. In the ensuing melee, Indians shot the stage driver, and soldiers, believing the innkeeper was an attacking Indian, shot him.

That evening Cochise and his band captured a wagon for additional hostages. The next day Cochise offered another trade, his hostages for Bascom's. Bascom refused unless the boy, who Cochise had never seen, was included. As this charade continued over several days, Bascom received reinforcements. Cochise felt the talks were a stall and withdrew from the area.

The hostages were left behind, all murdered and shockingly mutilated. When Bascom and his troops arrived on the scene, he ordered the six Apaches, and three additional Coyoteros, to be hung. Cochise, wrongly accused of the kidnapping, was now on the warpath.

Feeling fair dealings with the white man were impossible, Cochise spent the next twenty years exacting revenge. Before his capture, he killed ten white men for every Apache slain.

Continual harassment and encroachment by Spaniards in Apache territory, conflicts with the Comanche and Mexicans, American occupation of Apache ancestral lands– all of this proved more than the Apache could accept.

The great chiefs of the 1800's, Geronimo, Cochise, Mangus Coloradas, Nana, Loco and Victorio led their bands in raids and warfare against the white intruders. With the Apache, raiding had always been a way of life; the primary objective was to gather horses, cattle, food and clothing. In warfare, fighting the enemy was the main objective, although the Apache always collected plunder after a battle.

Although there were countless skirmishes between the Americans and the Apache during the mid to late 1800's, the final analysis found the Apache greatly overwhelmed by superior equipment, greater numbers and the use of their Indian brothers against them as scouts.

The Comanches began their rise to power in the Southwest around 1700. Increased mobility, provided by horses that had been introduced by the Spanish, extended the Comanche's range far beyond their traditional Wyoming homelands. They were horsemen without equal. Unlike other Indian tribes who would ride into battle and dismount to fight, the Comanches fought their campaigns mounted. They were quick to capture the livestock of the enemies they vanquished and they owned vast herds of horses. It was not uncommon to find warriors with more than 100 horses of their own. Raiding parties traveled as far as Mexico and would return with as many as 1,000 captured horses. By the mid 18th century Comanche were well established on the southern plains and played an important role in blocking the northward expansion of the Spanish, who they were able to successfully contain in southern Texas. The Spaniards grew so frustrated with the continual raiding by Comanches, they enlisted the aid of the Apaches in an attempt to drive them from Texas. The Spanish and Apache combined forces were defeated, with the Spanish driven to seek shelter in central Texas and the Apaches routed from the area.

Early in the 19th century, the Comanches occupied about 240,000 square miles of Texas, Colorado, Kansas, New Mexico and Oklahoma.

Above: Bean grinding holes along the Rio Grande, Big Bend National Park, Texas. Comanche and Apache Indians frequented the area in raids on white settlers until peace treaties were finally signed in the late 1880's.
PHOTO BY CARR CLIFTON

GERONIMO! LEGENDARY APACHE WARRIOR

The most famous Apache warrior, Geronimo led the Bedonkohe Apache from their region near the headwaters of the Gila River. Legendary for his bravery and tenacity, he was said, in numerous documented accounts, to have been clairvoyant. A story is told of Geronimo traveling home from a raid and suddenly saying to his band in a trance-like state, "Tomorrow afternoon, as we march back northward along the north side of the mountains, we will see a man standing on a hill to our left. He will howl to us and tell us that the troops have captured our base camp." The event occurred the next day just as Geronimo's vision predicted.

Geronimo never fully understand the nature of the white man, who would seize Apache land without regard for Indian rights. The whites, Geronimo often mused, would plunder Apache lands, steal their horses, kill their people and destroy their villages. Why then did the white man think it was so strange when the Apache responded in like measure?

In 1883, Geronimo surrendered to General George Crook, thought by most to be a fair, if somewhat harsh man. Upon taking office as the head of the Military Department in 1882, General Crook placed the blame for the Indian situation where it belonged. "Greed and avarice on the part of the Whites, in other words the almighty dollar, is at the bottom of nine-tenths of our Indian problems." Geronimo, though this first peace lasted only three years, wanted to end the conflicts with the white man.

In meeting General Crook the first time, Geronimo told Crook he believed that the Apache could fight indefinitely against the Mexicans, killing them by using rocks instead of rifles if need be, a chore that was not unpleasant to Geronimo, who had lost two wives and four children to the Spanish by the 1850's. But, he then explained to General Crook, once the Gray Fox (Crook) came, guided by his own people (Apache from other tribes), he knew that he must either make terms or die fighting.

General Crook made peace with Geronimo and granted favorable terms to the Apache. Unfortunately, Crook's terms were overridden in Washington and Geronimo, again betrayed by the white man, was back on the warpath.

In 1885, Geronimo was again raiding with a band of 35 warriors, eight boys, and 100 women and children. Geronimo and his band killed 75 civilians, 12 Indians of other tribes, two officers,

Geronimo in 1886.

eight soldiers and more than 100 Mexicans. Geronimo was wounded many times and lost six of his men, two boys, a woman and a child. The campaign was made possible by using guerrilla warfare, with Geronimo and his people striking in lightning fast raids, then retreating to the safety of their mountain strongholds.

By 1886, the United States Army had more than five thousand troops pursuing the last of the Apache bands, and on September 4, 1886, Geronimo, the last of the Apache leaders to be apprehended, surrendered his band to General Crook for the second and final time, thus ending the Apache wars.

General Crook offered Geronimo and his band terms of two years in confinement, to be served outside the territory, after which they would be allowed to return to the reservation and rejoin their families, where they would be free. But again, forces in Washington were not inclined to treat the Apache with honor and refused to honor Crook's terms to Geronimo. General Sheridan, with his typical disregard for promises made to Indians, insisted on an unconditional surrender, and the permanent imprisonment of the Apache band.

General Crook replied he could not go back on his word to Geronimo and quickly resigned his command. Geronimo was confined to prison in Florida until 1894, when his band was moved to the Indian reservation at Fort Sill, Oklahoma, where he remained until his death, from natural causes, on February 17, 1909.

The Spaniards, Apaches and Mexicans had proven unable to counteract the Comanche menace. In 1835, the Texans established the Texas Rangers, a small but incredibly tough militia. The Rangers fought the Comanche on their own terms, striking in raids when the Comanche least expected them, and began to turn the tide against Comanche domination of the region. As more Anglo-Americans began crossing Comanche territory on their way to the California gold fields in 1849, the Comanche were dealt their most serious blow by white intruders. This did not come from the forts built by the U.S. Army following the Mexican War of 1846, but from a cholera epidemic introduced by white prospectors. Comanches, who once numbered as many as 20,000, were decimated by the white man's disease, which killed about half their population. Comanche forces never fully recovered from the epidemic.

In the 1860's, Quanah Parker, the last of the great Comanche war chiefs, preyed on white settlers on the plains of Texas. The son of a white woman, Cynthia Ann Parker, who was captured by Comanches as a young girl, and a Comanche chief, Quanah's daring raids and close escapes from the U. S. Cavalry rekindled war fever among the Plains Indians who still remained free from reservation existences. Quanah was the most feared of all Comanche chiefs, and the most fearless. Peace did not come to the region until his surrender in 1875. His was the last Comanche band to surrender.

Quanah Parker proved himself to be a great leader in times of peace as well as times of war. He became a politician and financier who found ways to merge the interests of both

Above: North Rim, Grand Canyon National Park. The Paiutes populated regions of the Grand Canyon area, Colorado and southern Utah. The Utes are thought to be descendants of the Fremont culture. PHOTO BY JACK W. DYKINGA

the white men and his people. He searched for his mother, discovered her long dead, and then found solace living with her relatives who

taught him to read and write English, and the ways of the white man's world.

The Ute Indians of Colorado and the Paiutes of southern Utah are both related to Indians of the Great Basin tradition. Utes, thought to be descendants of the Fremont culture, are the longest reigning residents of Colorado. They were the largest tribe and had occupied a majority of the state's land. They are the only tribe with a reservation in Colorado.

The Utes are related to Paiutes, Comanches, Shoshones, and Bannocks. Each tribe speaks a Shoshonean language. They were known to trade with, and at times raid, the Pueblos to the south, and joined with Comanche relatives to drive the Apache from the Colorado plains in the 1800's. They later formed a close association with Jicarilla Apache, intermarrying and standing together against enemies.

The Utes had no conflicts with the Spanish, and often allied with them against Comanches and Navajos. When the Americans first entered their territory the Utes were unthreatened. By the mid 1800's, encroachment by settlers, and the presence of the U.S. Army, drove the Utes and their Jicarilla Apache allies to attack forts and settlements. This led to reprisals by the military and the Utes sought peace. The last wild buffalo were gone, killed in 1897 in Lost Park, Colorado. Miners of the Pike's Peak Gold Rush swarmed the region, and the Utes moved to Indian reservations, where the boundaries frequently changed as the white men broke promise after promise.

Right: Council Rocks, Cochise West Stronghold. Indian grinding holes dot granite boulders in the Dragoon Mountains in Coronado National Forest. PHOTO BY JACK W. DYKINGA

The Indian Traders

The first Anglos to encounter Southwestern Indian tribes were explorers, trappers and traders, who paved the way for frontiersmen and settlers that followed. In 1821, William Becknell led a trading expedition to Santa Fe. His goods promptly sold and he returned home to acquire additional trade items. Becknell's successive trips established the Santa Fe Trail.

Accounts by early traders led to the arrival of Anglo merchants. Bringing wagon loads of trade goods, cloth, cooking utensils, dry foods, tools, shoes, nails, knives, guns and alcohol, the merchants established a base of operations for those who followed and opened markets in the East for products supplied by the Indians.

In 1831, William and Charles Bent formed a company with Frenchman Ceran Saint Vrain, building a fort in the Arkansas River Valley of Colorado for their headquarters. They traded goods from St. Louis, Navajo blankets, Mexican horses and numerous other items. Their main operations were at the fort, now Bent's Old Fort National Historic Site, which was a neutral site where Indians, Mexicans and Americans were all welcome. It was a major meeting center and enjoyed a peaceful existence until commandeered in the Mexican War of 1846. After the war, Charles Bent was appointed the first U.S. governor of New Mexico. Bent was killed and

Above: Rug Trader's Room at Hubbell Trading Post National Historic Site, Arizona. John Lorenzo Hubbell established the trading post at Ganado in 1878. PHOTO BY GEORGE H. H. HUEY

scalped within months by his constituents in the 1847 Taos Rebellion.

John Lorenzo Hubbell established 24 trading posts in the Southwest. He was a friend to the Navajo, encouraging their weaving crafts and hiring a Mexican silversmith to teach them the art of jewelry making.

Southwestern Indian tribes are known throughout the world for the quality and craftsmanship of their unique arts and crafts. Pottery, basketry, jewelry, and woven goods created by Native American craftsmen contribute substantially to both the art world and the economies of the Southwestern tribes each year. Although most people are familiar with traditional crafts and designs, today a new generation of artisans is emerging among the Southwestern Indian tribes. They are more contemporary than their ancestors and are gaining considerable fame and admiration in the field of Indian arts and crafts, and in the art world in general.

The Hopi Indians are accomplished artisans and craftsmen. They are well known for their exquisite carvings of kachinas, watercolor paintings, basketry, pottery and silverwork. Hopi pottery is extremely well crafted and shows the strong influence of their roots in Anasazi and Mogollon cultures. The majority of Hopi pottery is produced on First Mesa.

Hopi silverwork designs have been evolving since the later part of the nineteenth century, but were originally inspired by contact with Zuñi and Navajo silversmiths. A Zuñi silversmith named Layande was responsible for training the first Hopi silversmith, Sikyatala, in the art of silver working in the late 1880's.

The fine quality of Hopi overlay jewelry stands on its own merits and is especially popular. Their overlay designs are sometimes fashioned after Hopi pottery and basketry designs, incorporating a wide variety of stylized elements, including some very popular animal motifs. Silverwork designs often include inlay work of turquoise and coral.

The use of silver has been a relatively new part of Hopi jewelry making. During the early 1900's, silver was extremely hard for Hopi craftsmen to obtain. Sometimes when they would run out of the precious metal, they would ride or walk to Winslow, Arizona, where they would "acquire" silverware from local restaurants. They would then take the silverware to the nearest railroad track, place it on the rails, and wait for the trains to compress the silver into a pliable material. Today, Hopi craftsmen are not faced with shortages of raw materials. Their fine designs and excellent craftsmanship have become quite successful in the marketplace, so Hopi jewelry makers of today use only the finest materials in the creation of their art.

The Hopi art of kachina, or katsina, making has its roots in the ceremonial kivas and the religion of the Hopi people and their Anasazi (Hisatsinom) ancestors. Kachina are believed to be supernatural beings who dwell in the mountains, lakes, and springs and bestow blessings on the Pueblo people. They are the spirits dwelling in all things. Most kachinas are benevolent in nature and are responsible for rain, successful crops, and good health; others are ogres, or demons, and represent disciplinary functions. Hopi legends tell of the kachina bringing gifts and teaching the Indians arts and crafts. The kachina taught some of the faithful their ceremonies, how to make masks and costumes, and permitted them, as long as they were pure of heart, to act

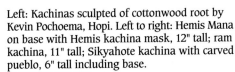

Left: Kachinas sculpted of cottonwood root by Kevin Pochoema, Hopi. Left to right: Hemis Mana on base with Hemis kachina mask, 12" tall; ram kachina, 11" tall; Sikyahote kachina with carved pueblo, 6" tall including base.
PHOTO BY JERRY JACKA
Courtesy: Steve Cowgill, Taos, New Mexico; McGees Beyond Native Tradition Gallery, Holbrook, Arizona

Right: An array of Southwestern Indian crafts. Left to right: wedding vase, 11" tall, by Minnie, Santa Clara Pueblo; wedding vase, 10" tall by T. Lewis, Hopi; Santo Domingo turquoise necklace; pottery jar, 8" tall, by Nathan Begay, Navajo; Zuni bracelet by L. Wayaco; deer kachina doll, 15" tall, by Cecil Miles, Jr., Hopi; Ganado red rug, 23" x 39" by Antonite Deswood, Navajo.
PHOTO BY JERRY JACKA
Courtesy The Heard Museum Gift Shop, Phoenix, Arizona

as if they were kachinas. If the ceremonies were enacted properly, the real kachinas would come and possess the masked dancers.

The kachinas are represented in various ways, all interconnected in the Pueblo peoples' minds. First, they are considered to be human, although they are not from this world. They are also the masked, costumed and painted dancers who appear in kivas and village plazas as impersonators of the spiritual kachinas to perform rites and ceremonies, which are artforms in themselves. Lastly, they are also the wooden figurines, small carved images of the life-sized beings, and they are revered by all the Pueblo people. The children use the figurines to study the ways of the kachina, and adults collect them in much the same manner Christians collect images of Christ on the Cross or statues of the Virgin Mary and their many saints. The incredible beauty and surrealistic properties of kachina carvings make them extremely popular with non-Indian art collectors as well.

The Navajo are an Athabascan people who migrated to the Southwest region from Canada more than 1,000 years ago. They were nomadic hunters and gatherers, and were not inclined to live in close knit villages like the Hopi and Pueblo Indians of the Southwest. An intelligent and creative people, the Navajo were

Above: Hopi kachina dolls by Seona. Left to right: Sipikne, 13" tall; Koshari Clown, 9" tall, Sio Hemis, 19" tall, Sakwa Hu, 15" tall.
PHOTO BY JERRY JACKA
Courtesy: The Heard Museum Gift Shop, Phoenix, Arizona

quick to learn the arts and crafts of the Pueblo Indians they encountered. The earlier Navajo weavings were primarily of cotton and natural fibers. Given the fragile nature of these fibers, little now remains of early Navajo woven crafts.

Even though hostile clashes between the Navajo and Pueblos were not uncommon, given the fierce raiding nature of the early Navajo, it was the Rio Grande Pueblo Indians who taught the Navajo how to weave the beautiful wool rugs that they are now famous for worldwide. After the Pueblo Revolt of 1680, many Rio Grande area Pueblo Indians fled west to the lands of the Hopi and Navajo to escape retaliation from the Spaniards.

Weaving in wool did not begin in the Southwest until sheep were introduced by the Spaniards about A.D. 1600. The oldest examples of Navajo weaving ever found were discovered in Massacre Cave in Canyon del Muerto, at Canyon de Chelly National Monument on the Navajo Reservation. They were found, in 1805, as the Spaniards inspected the cave after they had killed around 100 Navajo warriors, women and children.

Navajo arts of jewelry making and metal work are synonymous with silver and turquoise. The turquoise stone is believed, by Navajo and many other groups of people around the world, to possess benign powers that ward off calamities and many of life's hazards. Although metal work by the Navajo dates from the middle of the 19th century, all early work was done in iron or copper. The Navajo men learned the art of metal working when they were detained at Fort Sumner, after the "Long Walk" that marked the end of the Navajo's freedom to live as they pleased and incarcerated

THE ROLE OF THE KACHINA

The kachina, or katsina, are believed by the Pueblo Indians to be supernatural beings who dwell in mountains, lakes, and springs and bestow many blessings on the Pueblo people. Kachina are the spirits of all things, from the birds in the sky to the corn in the fields. Among the Zuñi people they are known as koko.

Most kachina are benevolent in nature and are responsible for rain, successful crops, and good health. Others are ogres, or demons, and are used to represent disciplinary functions. It is said that ogres will eat children who do not obey the kachinas, or do not behave themselves.

Kachinas, according to Pueblo legends, were real beings and would visit the Pueblo people when they were sad, or lonely, and would dance for them. The kachina brought gifts and taught the Indians arts and crafts, how to build their villages, cultivate crops, and hunt. As time went by, the Pueblo people began to take the kachina for granted and lost respect for their benevolence. Violent struggles broke out between the Pueblo Indians and the supernatural beings. Finally, the kachina quit visiting the Pueblos.

Because the kachina truly cared for the Pueblo people, they taught some of the faithful their ceremonies, how to make kachina masks and costumes, and permitted them, as long as they were pure of heart, to act as if they were the kachinas. If the kachina ceremony was enacted properly, real kachinas would then appear and take possession of the masked dancers.

Although all members of the Pueblo tribes are initiated into the Kachina Society, only men are allowed to impersonate the kachinas.

Kachinas are represented in various ways, all connected in the minds of the Pueblo people. First, they are considered to be human, although they are not; they are the masked, costumed and painted dancers who appear in kivas and village plazas as impersonators of the spiritual kachinas to perform rites and ceremonies; and they are the wooden figurines, small carved images of the life-sized beings, revered by all of the Pueblo people. Children use the figurines to study the ways of the kachina, and adults collect and display them in the same manner that many Christians collect images of Christ or statues of the Virgin Mary.

Right: Koshari clown kachinas by Regina Naha.
PHOTO BY JERRY JACKA

at the Bosque Redondo reservation in New Mexico. No silver work was fashioned until the Navajo returned to their homelands, the site of the present Navajo Reservation that occupies portions of northern Arizona, northwestern New Mexico and southeastern Utah.

Early production methods were crude and inefficient, but the quality and production of silver jewelry gradually increased. It was not until around 1880 that settings of any kind

Above: Zuñi fetishes. Fetishes of stone, shell and other materials have been used for centuries in connection with American Indian rituals. Today, they are also popular as collectibles and are often incorporated into jewelry. The fetish necklaces shown here are by contemporary Zuñi artisans Lavina Tsikewa and Annette Hannaweeka.
PHOTO BY JERRY JACKA

were made, then bits of glass, beads and garnets were introduced into Navajo silverwork designs. Around 1900, turquoise began to appear in increasing quantities and thereafter became closely associated with the Navajo silverwork designs.

A wide range of silver articles are currently produced by the Navajo: conchas for belts, buttons, rings, earrings, bracelets, necklaces, hat bands and more. The influence of other tribes and cultures can be seen in the Navajo work. Conchas strung on belts were inspired by the silver disks that hung from the belts of Plains Indian women. The most common type of necklace is made of large, hollow, silver beads that are separated by flower shaped pendants. These are commonly called "squash blossom" necklaces because of the pendant

Right: These pottery figurines represent variations of the popular storyteller motif. The one at the left is by J. Pecos and the smallest one, which is only 3" tall, is by Rose Pecos. Both potters are from the Jemez Pueblo. Cochiti potter Vangie Suina made the two at the right.
PHOTO BY JERRY JACKA

feature. The squash blossom design copied the pomegranate blossoms that were formerly used to adorn Spanish clothing and saddlery, but these designs have been used so extensively by the Navajo that they are now considered to be traditional Navajo jewelry designs.

The Zuñi are accomplished silver workers. In addition, they craft the majority of fetishes used by Southwestern Indians. Fetishes are objects in which it is believed spirits live; they are thought to have the ability to give their owners supernatural powers. Use of fetishes dates to prehistoric times. Ownership of fetishes is held by individuals, clans, societies or kivas.

Above: A mixed group of Indian jewelry-Navajo, Hopi and Zuni.
PHOTO BY JERRY JACKA   Courtesy: Keams Canyon Arts and Crafts, Arizona

The fetishes most prized by the Indians are those that are naturally formed and shaped like animals. These items may be of stone, shell, antler or other materials. Fetishes that are carved by Zuñi fetish makers are highly respected by other tribes. They are often adorned with small bits of shell, turquoise and coral, as this is thought to increase their powers.

Although they were once accomplished in all forms of arts and crafts, silver jewelry represents the great majority of Zuñi crafts produced today. Basketry and weaving are rarely practiced, and pottery is produced on a diminished scale, as are kachinas.

Pueblo Indians, and their ancestors in the Southwest, have been producing pottery for nearly two thousand years. The earliest pots

were utility wares that served to increase the quality of life by providing better storage than baskets, and by being easier to cook with. As the shapes, styles and techniques used in pottery making evolved, it was not long before Indian women began to decorate their wares, and individuals within the same group often used the same designs. Although work of a single craftsman can sometimes be found and identified among items in prehistoric finds, it was not until earlier this century that Pueblo Indians began to sign their pottery, signifying a change to individual styles.

In addition to the fine pottery produced by the Hopi, excellent pottery is produced by many other Pueblo Indians. Acoma produces fine traditional pottery, in addition to creations

that blend traditional designs with exciting new techniques and materials. At Zia Pueblo, traditional pottery making is still practiced, with distinctive designs in red clay and mineral black that often feature a bird motif. Jemez and Santo Domingo Pueblos also produce pottery with traditional designs.

In 1895, Lesou, a Hopi Indian from Hano on First Mesa, who was a member of the Jesse Fewkes Expedition of the same year, brought his wife, Nampeyo, pieces of prehistoric Hopi pottery found at Sikatki and Awatovi. Nampeyo incorporated these ancient designs into her pottery and to this day their descendants have carried on this style, with all their work being known as Nampeyo Hopi pottery. Work by Joy Navasie features a white slip decorated with natural mineral red and black designs that have become extremely popular. This style originated with Joy's mother, Frog Woman (Paqua), and is carried on by Joy's daughters.

At San Ildefonso and San Carlos Pueblos, pottery designs have become decidedly more contemporary during this century. At San Ildefonso Pueblo, highly polished red and black wares with matte designs, and carved wares have long been popular. The work of Blue

Above: Baskets of Arizona Indian tribes. Back row: Left is Hopi with a 14" diameter; right is a 15" diameter Navajo. Front row (left to right): Tohono O'odham, 10" diameter and 9" diameter, Hopi, 14" diameter.
PHOTO BY JERRY JACKA
Art Courtesy of The Heard Museum Gift Shop, Phoenix, Arizona

Corn has evolved into several styles that meld traditional designs with a contemporary style that often incorporates backgrounds of white, red and orange.

Santa Clara Pueblo pottery is similar in design to San Ildefonso styles and is often decorated with animal and bird motifs. Several exceptional potters, producing highly collectable art, are found at Santa Clara. Laguna Pueblo produces pottery similar to Acoma, but normally with heavier walls and art that is not as carefully executed. The Acoma Pueblo pottery has the thinnest walls and lightest weights of modern Pueblo Indian pottery. The Cochiti Pueblo is famous for pottery that is often shaped in the form of birds, and for humorous figures styled to represent people and animals.

Some pottery is still being produced by non-Pueblo Indians, including the Tohono O'otham (Papago), Navajo, Maricopa and others, but are generally utility wares that are not highly decorated.

NAVAJO RUG WEAVING

The Navajo learned the art of weaving from Pueblo Indians fleeing the Rio Grande Valley of New Mexico after the Pueblo Revolt of 1680. The Pueblo Indians are thought to have either joined the Navajo to escape possible retribution from the Spaniards, or possibly they were captured by the Navajo during their flight to safety.

The Navajo acquired sheep from early Spanish colonists and were adept herdsmen, their semi-nomadic lifestyle being perfectly suited to raising sheep and cattle. During the early years of Navajo weaving, designs primarily were copied from those of their Pueblo teachers. They were simple in concept and in their use of color. Most were comprised of stripes in natural sheep colors: black, brown, white and gray. The grays were achieved by carding black and white wools together. The early Navajo woven goods were designed mainly as dresses and blankets.

The Navajo have always been a bright and creative people and soon began to elaborate on the designs of their Pueblo teachers. Geometric designs were soon introduced and the range of colors amplified by the use of vegetal dyes. Indigo blue dye, introduced by the Spaniards, and cochineal red cloth the Spaniards supplied (which the Navajo unraveled and respun into yarn) soon added two important elements to Navajo woven designs. During the 1700's and 1800's, Navajo blankets were widely respected for their quality and were a sought after trade product by the Indian, Spanish and Anglo-American traders who found eager markets for Navajo goods.

During the late 1880's, the market for Navajo blankets became saturated as cheaper, softer

Above: Teec Nos Pos design Navajo rug, 46" x 64", by Evelyn Yazzie, Navajo.
PHOTO BY JERRY JACKA   Courtesy of Margaret Kilgore Gallery, Scottsdale, Arizona

blankets produced by woolen mills replaced the demand for hand woven Navajo products. Traders then demanded thicker woven products, often with borders to frame Navajo designs, that could be used for rugs.

Navajo designs are named for the area in which they are produced. Two Grey Hills, Lukachukai, Three Turkey Ruin, Crystal, Black Mountain, Teec Nos Pos and Ganado areas all produce designs distinct in colors and pattern. In the Shiprock area, sand painting designs are incorporated into Yei and Yeibechai rugs. Sand painting designs, considered sacred, are altered by weavers to allow their use for commercial purposes.

Left: A Ganado Red style Navajo woven rug by Sarah Begay, Navajo.
PHOTO BY JERRY JACKA
Courtesy of Keams Canyon Arts & Crafts, Arizona

Basket making pre-dates the invention of pottery in the Southwest. The earliest Indians used woven baskets to gather and store foods. A variety of designs were made, including baskets that were lined with a coating of pitch which made them water-tight for cooking foods. Cooking with baskets was generally accomplished by placing heated stones inside baskets that contained food. Although this resulted in a great number of baskets being burned, it was a better process than warming some items directly over a flame.

Among most tribes of the Southwest, basket making is slowly disappearing as a viable commercial endeavor. Countless hours needed to create tightly woven baskets are rarely

Above: Baskets and basketry materials used by Annie Antone, Tohono O'odham. Upper and lower left: yucca. Far right (green): bear grass, whole and stripped. Lower center (red): roots of banana yucca. Upper (black): Devil's Claw, whole and stripped, in bundle at left.
PHOTO BY JERRY JACKA
Courtesy C & R Traders, Casa Grande, Arizona

rewarded financially. The Tohono O'otham (Papago) produce more baskets than any other tribe in the United States. Baskets are used in a number of Indian ceremonies by Hopi, Navajo, Apache and other tribes. Baskets are still in demand by some tribes that have now ceased making their own baskets, even though they are no longer quite as popular with many non-Indian buyers as they once were.

The Hopi Indians of Arizona still produce tightly woven coiled baskets, bowls, plaques and containers that are quite beautiful. They also produce plaited yucca sifter baskets on all three of their mesas.

The Apache, although once famous for fine basketry, now produce only a more utilitarian ware. Several other Southwestern Indian tribes also produce a limited number of baskets, most of which are relatively plain in design and are normally for their own use.

Seri Indians, of northwest Mexico along the Sea of Cortez, produce good quality coiled baskets that are often found in stores throughout the Southwest. The import items are popular with both Native American tribes and with non-Indian buyers. The region the Seri occupy is actually similar in all ways to the Southwestern United States and, except for the international boundary, would today be considered a region of the Southwest. The Seri are perhaps most famous for their carved ironwood figures, which they only began producing during the 1960's. The Seri had been fishermen until Mexican shrimp boats destroyed Seri fishing areas. Seri carvers had long been using the ironwood found in their area to make different types of tools, musical instruments, bowls, kitchen utensils and other items. Without their fishing grounds to provide income and sustenance for the tribe, the Seri began to carve ironwood figures of birds, fish, and animals, carvings that were immediately popular with visitors to their area. During the late 1960's, Seri art began to be exported to the United States, where it has been well accepted.

Above: Pottery group by Dorothy Torivio, Acoma Pueblo, New Mexico. Tallest: 8". Far left: 4" diameter. Far right: 3 1/2" tall.
PHOTO BY JERRY JACKA

Below: Pueblo Indian pottery with animal motifs. Left to right: Deer, 8" tall, by P. Romero of Jemez Pueblo; Lizard, 3" diameter by P. Iule, Acoma; Bird, 5" tall, by Volanda Trujillo, Acoma; Wedding vase, by Reycita Cosen of Santa Clara Pueblo.
PHOTO BY JERRY JACKA
Art Courtesy of The Heard Museum Gift Shop, Phoenix, Arizona